HUMAN SERVICE DELIVERY TO
Latinos

KRISTI KANEL

D1457009

ISBN: 978-1-60250-043-3
         1-60250-043-6

59 Damonte Ranch Parkway, Suite B284 • Reno, NV 89521 • (800) 970-1883

www.benttreepress.com

Address all correspondence and order information to the above address.

TABLE OF CONTENTS

ABOUT THE AUTHOR

Dr. Kristi Kanel earned her Ph.D. in Counseling Psychology from the University of Southern California, Masters in Counseling from California State University, Fullerton, and Bachelor of Science degree in Human Services from California State University, Fullerton. She is currently an Associate Professor in the Department of Human Services at California State University, Fullerton.

Her work with Latinos in Southern California spans the last 25 years. She has provided counseling services to Latinos as individuals, couples, families, and in groups. Dr. Kanel has worked at nonprofit agencies, government agencies, and in the private sector. In all of these settings, Dr. Kanel has specialized in the treatment of Latinos.

Specifically, she has worked extensively with Latinos in which child abuse and spousal abuse were major problems. During her career as a psychotherapist, she has also treated many Latino-specific issues, such as Ataque de Nervios, for which she has recently conducted a large research project. She has dealt with issues related to Santeria and the use of Curanderos, gangs among adolescents, and other issues related to acculturation stress.

Dr. Kanel is bilingual but not Latina herself. She has conducted research with Latinos from the community in order to examine the specific mental health needs of this group. As mentioned above, she has also conducted research into the phenomenon referred to as Ataque de Nervios. Both of these studies and the results will be presented in this book.

Her most recent focus with this population has been in the area of ESL college students and possible accommodations for them. Dr. Kanel became interested in this issue as the number of ESL students enrolled in her own university classes began to increase in the past decade. She is extremely interested in ensuring that the Latino community receives human services from educated people who are bilingual, and in order for this to happen, it is important that bilingual/bicultural students be assisted in completing their college programs.

PREFACE

Overview

This book was created as a result of the increasing numbers of Latinos using human services in the United States. Latinos make up the largest percentage of minorities in the country, and it is imperative that human service workers understand the most effective interventions when working with this population.

This book provides the reader with theoretical and practical ideas about how to most appropriately serve Latinos. The focus is on working with Latinos in which Spanish is the primary language. When Spanish is the dominant language, it is believed that Latino culture, rather than American culture, is more influential on the life of the individual and the family.

This book examines Latino culture, compares it to American culture, and offers practical suggestions on how to intervene with Latinos who are influenced by Latino culture.

Although it is not expected that every human service worker be bilingual, the author has included in the appendix a brief English-to-Spanish dictionary with words commonly used by human service workers when providing services to Spanish-speaking clients. The reader is encouraged to become familiar with these terms and practice using them when possible. They help to bridge the gap between client and helper.

Throughout the book, the author has bold-faced certain terms. These terms will be defined at the end of each chapter in a glossary.

CHAPTER CONTENT

Chapter 1: Introduction to Latinos and Culture

This chapter discusses why it is important to study Latinos as a population using human services. Prevalence rates are presented, along with general cultural considerations when working with Latinos. Additionally, general definitions of culture are explored.

Chapter 2: Latino Culture in the United States

This chapter examines the specific issues, needs, and cultural aspects of Latinos. Specific aspects of Mexican culture, Puerto Rican culture, and Cuban culture are addressed.

Chapter 3: Mental Health Delivery to Latinos

This chapter takes a look at how Latino values differ from mainstream cultural values in the field of mental health. Kanel's research study is examined regarding the mental health needs of Latinos. Other factors related to mental health issues, such as cultural patterns, acculturation, and ethnicity identity formation, are discussed. Mental health treatment is examined as related to Latinos.

Chapter 4: Special Issues Facing Latinos in the United States

This chapter examines specific mental health problems and other social issues that Latinos often face as related to human services. Kanel's study on Ataque de Nervios is presented in detail. Also discussed is teenage pregnancy, gangs, substance abuse, domestic violence, and AIDS.

Chapter 5: Social Welfare Delivery to Latinos

This chapter addresses issues related to child protection and abuse, needs of the elderly, and financial assistance. Specific issues related to Latinos and intervention are discussed.

Chapter 6: The Educational System and Latinos

In this chapter, American educational values are compared with Latino values. This serves as a foundation for understanding educational achievement among Latinos. The chapter concludes with a discussion on how to assist Latinos to perform better in educational institutions.

Appendix A: *Questionnaire: Perceived Mental Health Needs of Latinos in Orange County.* (This is the survey used in Kanel's study about mental health needs of Latinos.)

Appendix B: *Questionnaire: Ataque de Nervios* (This is the survey used in Kanel's study on Ataque de Nervios.)

Appendix C: *English-to-Spanish Dictionary*
Though not exhaustive, this brief translation dictionary may be helpful for some.

SPECIAL FEATURES

Each chapter concludes with a glossary of terms that have been bold-faced throughout the chapter. A reference list is provided at the end of each chapter for easy access, as well.

CHAPTER 1

Introduction to Latinos and Culture

INTRODUCTION

Throughout the United States over the last 20 years, there has been an increasing need for human service workers to develop competency in providing services to Spanish-speaking families. Undoubtedly, people from many Latino backgrounds have been using mental health services, social welfare services, and educational services regularly. Much has been written about how these services should be modified to meet the special needs of this population. In order to most effectively serve Latino families, human service workers at all levels should obtain knowledge and skills relevant to the history and cultural norms of families in which Spanish is the dominant language.

PREVALENCE OF LATINOS

Many agencies and researchers have conducted surveys to help understand the needs of Spanish-speaking families; this research also includes basic facts about the number of Spanish speakers or Latinos in the community.

Across the Nation

According to the U.S. Bureau of the Census (2003), as of 2002, there were 40 million people of Hispanic/Latino identification living in the United States (not including Puerto Rico). As of 2000, 10,459,616 (31.6% of the total California population) were residing in California. Texas housed the next most, with

6,669,666, then New York with 2,867,583, Florida with 2,682,715, Illinois with 1,530,262, Arizona with 1,295,617, and New Mexico with 765,386 (42.1% of total state population) (U.S. Census, 2001). It is probable that the type of Latino background found in each of these states differs due to migration patterns affected by proximity of native country. The fact that certain U.S. states and communities have well-established Latino areas also facilitates immigrants' transitions from their native countries to the U.S. For example, Mexicans are more likely to migrate to California and Texas because Mexico borders these states, and these states have many predominantly Spanish-speaking communities where Mexican cultural traditions are common. Cubans migrate more to Florida because it is close to Cuba and because Cuban cultural traditions and businesses abound in Miami. Puerto Ricans tend to migrate to New York because certain neighborhoods in and around New York City are largely populated by Puerto Ricans, which increases feelings of comfort among those immigrating for work, school, or family.

Latinos make up the greatest percentage of immigrants and are the fastest-growing and youngest group of immigrants. The median age of Latinos in the U.S. is only 25.3 compared to the national median age in the U.S. which is 35.3. In Arizona, 36% of Latinos are under age 18. Overall, older Hispanics (those 65 years and older) make up 5.3% of the U.S. population compared to non-Hispanic elderly, who make up 14% of the U.S. population. Latina women make up 12% of the overall U.S. population, with a median age of 29.1 versus 36.6 for the overall female population. Women of Mexican descent are at the top of the list in regard to birth rates for women between the ages of 15-44 (Arredondo, p. 2006).

The California Trend

In 1990, 568,000 (Orange County Register, p. 17) Hispanics resided in Orange County (a large county in southern California that attracts many Hispanics because of its proximity to Mexico). By 2000, the total Latino population in this county was 801,796, which is 29% of the 2,760,948 people living in this county (U.S. Census Bureau, 2001). In fact, in Santa Ana, a city located in central Orange County, 76% of the total population is Latino (Becerra & Alvarez, 2001). The number of Latinos residing in Orange County—and throughout the U.S.—is probably greater than the Census reflects because many Latinos living in the U.S. are not authorized to be here, so they are afraid to report their residence in a government census. An alternative method for grasping the true prevalence of Latinos in Orange County is to review the number of Latinos enrolled in public schools, which in the school year 1998-1999 was 40%, while White enrollment was 43%, Asian was 12%, and Other was 5%. This indicates that Latinos are approaching the White population level in that area. Another study showed that in Orange County, Latino births climbed from fewer than 9,100 in 1984 to 23,000 babies per year from 1992 to 1996, while White births declined, and Asian and Black births plateaued (Orange County Register, 1999, p. 17).

Los Angeles County also houses a large percentage of Latinos; in particular, East Los Angeles has the highest concentration of Latinos in the U.S. (an estimated 96.8% of its residents are Latino (Becerra & Alvarez, 2001). While New York City was the U.S. city with the most Latinos in numbers (2.16 million), as indicated by responses on the 2000 U.S. Census, Latinos make up only 27% of the total population of that city. On the other hand, Latinos make up 47% of the population in Los Angeles (McDonnell, 2001).

In a survey conducted in 1997 (Mental Health Association), it was discovered that many human service workers perceived a strong need for bilingual human service workers in Los Angeles County. Out of the 54 workers surveyed, 38.9% said there was a very large need for bilingual workers, 13% said a large need, and 31.5% said a moderate need. Only 7.4% said there was no need for bilingual human service workers. When asked the language of greatest need, 40.7% said Spanish, while 5.6% said Korean, 3.7% said Chinese, and 3.7% said Other. The workers also seemed to feel there was a need for more bicultural workers, as 71% said there was a moderate to very large need for human service workers who were bicultural. Out of African-Americans, Asian Pacific Islanders, Native Americans, and Hispanics, 78.3% said that the need for bicultural workers was for Hispanics. Eighty-six percent of those surveyed said this need will increase.

In light of these results, those of us in the human service profession can expect a growing demand for culturally sensitive and competent providers to the Latino community. Of course the need is probably strongest in California, where the number of Latinos is highest, but other states must also understand the special needs and adopt the effective interventions required for this group.

WHAT IS CULTURE?

Before examining Latino culture and the corresponding special needs, a brief discussion about culture in general may be helpful. According to Hogan-Garcia (2003, p. 19-20), a **culture** or **ethnic group** (terms used interchangeably) is a group in which members share common cultural heritage made up of values, beliefs, attitudes, and customs related to language, religion, and family life processes. Hogan-Garcia suggests that understanding culture as multilevel is the first skill for human service workers endeavoring to be culturally competent. The aspects of culture involved in this multilevel model include language and communication, family life processes, healing beliefs and practices, religion, art and expressive forms, diet/foods, recreation, clothing, history, social status factors, and social group interaction patterns (p. 21).

In addition to a culture based on ethnicity, there is also a culture found in the agencies and workers that serve people of various cultures. This **organizational culture** will be referred to as the **mainstream culture** and refers to the norms, policies, procedures, programs, and processes that organizations employ (Hogan-Garcia, 2003. p. 21). One of the central reasons for learning how to provide human services to Spanish-speaking families is that the organizational culture often serves this population ineffectively due to differences in customary ways and belief patterns. In subsequent chapters, some of the discrepancies between mainstream culture and Latino culture will be discussed. It is hoped this discussion will increase awareness about potential barriers for effective human service delivery to this population. Barriers to effective communication—and therefore barriers to effective intervention—include language, nonverbal communication errors and misperceptions, stereotypes and preconceptions, personal stress factors, and organizational policies unfriendly to cultural diversity (Hogan-Garcia, 1999, p. 43). These factors will be included in discussions throughout the text.

GENERAL CULTURAL CONSIDERATIONS WITH LATINOS

Language

One cannot assume that all people of Latino origin speak Spanish. However, the focus of this book is on people who do speak Spanish or who are raised in homes in which Spanish is the dominant language. It is in these homes that Latino culture is probably most evident. Language has been proposed as a large determinant of culture. The well-known linguistic **Sapir-Whorf Theory** proposes, "If we define culture as what a society does and thinks, then the thought aspects of different cultures are strongly conditioned by their particular languages." It goes on to say, "Language determines culture through the particular contents of the concepts that make up the world of things in which the culture is interested"(Sapir, 1921, p. 219). For example, the use of masculine and feminine words in Spanish may indicate that this is a culture in which gender holds a strong place in determining cultural behaviors (indeed, there is a strong history of chauvinism in Spanish cultures). Another example can be found in the Hopi Indian language, which does not have a grammatical distinction of time as we know it, but instead distinguishes by degrees of intensity. Because of this language difference, Whorf found that he and a Hopi could not discuss the "same world" (Whorf, B., 1956, p. 216).

Another language factor has to do with its ability to motivate people to integrate into mainstream culture. Those people whose primary language is Spanish have a difficult time integrating into the larger society when they do not learn to speak English. People who are motivated to integrate into mainstream society are more likely to learn English than those who do not feel the need to integrate (Kanel, 2000a). Language is often a major obstacle when human service workers try to provide services to Spanish-speaking families. Without a common language, the worker and client cannot understand each other. Another potential problem occurs when human service workers attempt to encourage Spanish speakers to learn English as a way to improve communication between them. If these clients do not wish to learn English, and if the worker continues to force it on the client, the situation can become frustrating for both the client and the worker. As Kanel proposes, motivation to acquire a new language is two-fold, **integrative** and **instrumental.** Integrative motivation refers to a desire to become acculturated to mainstream ideas and to fully assimilate into American culture. Instrumental motivation refers to the practical aspects of learning English, such as being able to understand coworkers and carry out banking and shopping activities, etc. Unless the worker can convince the client that learning English would be instrumental to him or her in daily life or until the client expresses desire to integrate into mainstream culture, then focusing on new language acquisition is futile.

As can be learned from previously mentioned prevalence rates of Latinos, being bilingual would no doubt be extremely helpful to human services providers. Communication barriers can be broken down this way, and a better understanding between client and helper can be formed. By human service workers learning a little bit about the Spanish language, it is possible that overall better communication and understanding between client and helper will be accomplished, and more effective service delivery will be possible.

Personalismo

Personalismo refers to the cultural pattern of relating to others in a personal manner that may include exaggerated warmth, emotions, and strong need for rapport in order to experience safety or trust. In English, the word "personalism" is not often used, perhaps because it is not a necessity in our society; indeed, excessive closeness may be considered a hindrance in mainstream American business culture, which is more task-oriented than person-oriented. It is particularly important for human service workers to grasp the idea of personalismo when working with Spanish-speaking families because developing trust is essential to the helping relationship. This may mean that time will be spent in seemingly idle chitchat about topics unrelated to the task at hand, but helpers should focus on developing rapport first, in order to respect the Latino need for personalismo.

Affiliative and Cooperative

The mainstream American culture has a long history in **individualism** and competition. In part, the capitalistic economy has reinforced these values; in a sense, it's "every man for himself." American culture values ambition and "getting ahead." Traditional Hispanic culture has focused instead on affiliative and cooperative behavior for survival. Probably due to high rates of poverty, Hispanics tend to help each other survive during economic hard times by encouraging multifamily dwelling, or finding jobs for one another, or giving money to each other.

Human service workers who might otherwise impose a more competitive value on this population must give this concept important notice. It is particularly important for educators to understand the lack of competitiveness among students at school.

Dependence and Family Enmeshment

Familism is the concept that deals with the Latino's loyalty to the family above all else. Members of a family see the family as the most important social unit. This may lead to problems for individual members at times, especially when work or school needs interfere with family needs.

Often, Latinos have been described as having an **enmeshed** family structure. Rather than having rigid boundaries between generations, parents may share personal feelings and needs with their children, and even expect children to take care of those needs. Likewise, children often lack a sense of privacy from their parents. Overall, there is a sense that all family members' feelings, beliefs, and needs are shared by all, and everyone in the family must take these needs and feelings into consideration when making decisions. While privacy and independence may be lost in these families, a sense of support and belonging remains strong with this type of structure.

Parenting Patterns

Parenting behaviors, like most cultures, are passed down from generation to generation. A democratic style of parenting is uncommon in Latino families. Instead, obedience is expected by the parents based on **respeto** (respect). Respeto implies an assumed acknowledgment that parents have the ultimate say and know what is best for the children, and children obey out of respect and duty. Respect is based both on gender and age. The father receives most of the respect. He considers himself to be the provider and main disciplinarian of the family, while the mother is the primary nurturer and caretaker of the children. She may, at times, secretly supersede his authority but will always allow him to save face in front of the children to ensure his **machismo** is maintained. The mother is often idealized and maintains a status of **marianismo** in which she is the ever-self-sacrificing good mother. Machismo and marianismo will be discussed in depth in Chapter 2.

Marital Patterns

Latino marital relationships can be thought of as **complementary**, that is, based on difference of power rather than equality. The relationship between husband and wife is often formal, which preempts intimacy or overt expression of anger. The man is expected to be aggressive, sexually experienced and protective, while the woman is to be virtuous, devoted to home and children, humble, and submissive. These attributes were influenced by the Spaniards' tradition of **chauvinism,** brought to the Americas during the Age of Discovery. Children validate the marriage, and the relationship between the parents and children is more important than marital functions. Romance is secondary to the preservation of the marriage, and divorce is rare. Even if couples choose not to live together, they often do not divorce.

Religion

Catholicism has been the major religious choice of most Latinos since the Spaniards brought it to Central and South America in the 1500s. Interestingly, the natives of these lands, primarily Aztecs, Mayans, and Yaquis practiced spirituality through sorcery, animism, and other so-called primitive practices. Much of these practices became intertwined with Roman Catholicism. **Santeria**, the using of saints and statues, potions, and cantations, has been widely practiced by many Latinos. It often carries with it a dark side, sometimes bordering on voodoo. In fact, voodoo practices are not uncommon among some Puerto Ricans and Cubans who were heavily influenced by African culture.

The strength of Catholicism in the Hispanic community is thought to be one of the barriers between Hispanics and the predominantly Protestant communities of the southwest part of the United States (Schaefer, 1988, p. 311). However, the size and bureaucracy of the Catholic Church, and the fact that it has not done much for the Chicano movement politically, is probably the reason that many Latinos are shifting their loyalties to the more family-like atmospheres of the Protestant churches. For example, Jehovah's Witness meeting halls, Calvary Churches, and Mormon churches offer more cultural events and a more-personal atmosphere. The ministers and pastors often have the special charisma that attracts Latinos and makes them feel at home.

In a 2001 survey (Lobdell), Latinos were asked a variety questions about religious and political issues. The results indicate, "with each passing generation, more Latinos become Protestants. However, immigrants replenish the numbers of the Catholic church in the U.S." (Source: Tomas Rivera Policy Institute, 2001). In fact, 18% of first-generation Latinos identify themselves as Protestant compared with 32% of third-generation Latinos. Overall, the survey suggests that of the 40 million Latinos in the U.S., 70% are Catholic and 22% are Protestant. Other information obtained from this survey shows that 95% of Latinos have some religious affiliation and 45% attend church regularly. Of those who do not describe themselves as Catholic, 51% considered themselves evangelical Christians.

Interestingly, 56% of those who attend church want their congregation to be more active in social, educational, and political issues, and 74% believed that the church should provide assistance to illegal immigrants.

CHAPTER SUMMARY

It has been shown that the number of Latinos living in the United States is on the rise. They are primarily located in six states: California, Texas, Arizona, New York, Florida, and New Mexico. Many are non-English speaking, living in poverty, and residing here illegally. These factors affect their psychological and social functioning. In order for human service workers to effectively work with this fast-growing population, cultural sensitivity and knowledge is essential. Understanding how language differences, family structure, individual characteristics, and religion differ from mainstream cultural norms is helpful in providing appropriate interventions. While there are certain patterns that connect Hispanics, there are many differences between various Latino groups. These will be explored in Chapter 2.

GLOSSARY OF TERMS

Affiliative: a concept referring to the Latino tendency to engage in cooperative behaviors with others rather than to compete.

Chauvinism: a pattern of behavior in which the man is the protector of the family and is aggressive and experienced sexually.

Complementary: a marital structure based on difference of power rather than equality.

Culture: typically refers to a group in which members share common ethnic heritage made up of values, beliefs, attitudes, language, religion, customs, and family patterns.

Enmeshed: a common Latino family structure that tends to emphasize sharing and dependency among all family members.

Ethnic Group: a term often used interchangeably with "culture" that refers to a group of people who share cultural heritage, sometimes based on racial identity and language.

Familism: a concept that refers to the Latino value of loyalty to the family above all else.

Individualism: the American value of every man for himself.

Instrumental Motivation: the idea that suggests people may be motivated to acquire a new language because it helps them with the practical aspects of daily life.

Integrative Motivation: the idea that suggests people may be motivated to acquire a new language because it assists them in integrating into the culture.

Machismo: a concept that refers to the value of the man being strong, virile, and protective.

Mainstream Culture: the norms and standards of acceptable behavior that are often imposed on American citizens by various institutions.

Marianisma: the concept that refers to the value placed on the mother being self-sacrificing and idealized.

Organizational Culture: the norms, policies, procedures, and processes that are part of agencies and other organizations.

Personalismo: the Latino value of relating to others in a personal, warm manner and a strong need for rapport and trust.

Respeto: the Latino parenting value of complete obedience by children to show respect and duty to the parents.

Santeria: a religious practice in which saints are worshipped and potions, incantations, and sometimes voodoo is practiced.

Sapir-Whorf Theory: a theory that suggests that language determines culture.

REFERENCES

Arredondo, P. (2006). Working with Contemporary Latino Families. Presentation given at the Brief Therapy Conference in Anaheim, CA.

Becerra, H., & Alvarez, F. (2001). Latinos make big census gains. *Los Angeles Times.* May 10, 2001.

Hogan-Garcia, M. (2003). *The Four Skills of Cultural Diversity Competence.* Belmont, CA: Brooks/Cole Publishing.

Kanel, Kim. (2000a). "The Linguistics of Cultural Sensitivity." Presentation given at California State University, Fullerton. Fullerton, CA.

Lobdell, W. (2001). Latinos' Changing Church Patterns. *The Orange County Register.* May 5, 2001.

McDonnell, P. J. (2001). Mexicans change face of U.S. demographics. *Los Angeles Times.* May 5, 2001.

Mental Health Association of Los Angeles. (1997). "Human Resource Needs Assessment: Human Services Industry." Los Angeles, CA: Author.

Orange County Register. (1999). Sunday Edition, April 4. Front page, page 7. Author.

Sapir, E. (1921). *Language: An Introduction to the Study of Speech.* New York: Harcourt, Brace & World, Inc.

Schaefer, R. T. (1988). *Racial and Ethnic Groups 3rd Ed.* Illinois: Scott, Foresman and Company.

U.S. Bureau of the Census. (2003). *Statistical Abstract of the United States.* Washington, D.C.

U.S. Bureau of the Census. (2001). *Statistical Abstract of the United States.* Washington, D.C.

Whorf, B. (1956). "Science and Linguistics," in J. B. Carroll, ed., *Language, Thought and_Reality: Selected Writings of Benjamin Lee Whorf* (Cambridge, Mass: M.I.T. Press, p. 216).

CHAPTER 2

Latino Culture in the United States

HISPANICS/LATINOS

Whether we use the term "Hispanic," "Latino," or "Spanish descent," we are referring to people whose culture was influenced by the Spanish conquerors of the fifteenth and sixteenth centuries. Most of these Spaniards settled in Central and South America. The "Hispanic" label combines the offspring of colonized natives, the **Hispanos**, with the descendants of foreigners and political and economic refugees under one ethnic umbrella (Schaefer, 1988, p. 287). "Latino" is a term that comes from the usage of "Latin America" to refer to Central and South America. While there are differences among the various Latino groups, certain similarities exist, as well. The most notable thing they all have in common is the Spanish language. As has already been suggested by the Sapir-Whorf Theory, language influences thoughts and behaviors in a culture; therefore, there will no doubt be many similarities in customs due to this language. There will also be Spanish cultural influence evident in many patterns, since it was the Spaniards who first impacted the natives' experience and created the mixture of European thought with Native-American thought. Many of the customs and patterns observed in Latinos living in the U.S. today have a history rooted in Spain-based customs and norms.

Remember, despite differences in migration patterns and other historical facts, most Latino individuals have been strongly influenced by their Spaniard heritage, and the issues discussed for each of the Latino groups in this chapter may apply to Latinos from South American and Central American countries, as well. This chapter provides only a brief sketch of the migration patterns of Mexican-Americans, Cuban-Americans, and Puerto Ricans and typical cultural norms that may separate them from each other.

MEXICANS-AMERICANS

Individuals of Mexican origin are by far the largest ethnic group in the United States (Schaefer, 1988, p. 286), as well as the largest group of Hispanics in this country. They have heavily populated the Southwest region of the U.S., as this area was once part of Mexico. Mexican-Americans have been referred to as **Chicanos,** particularly in the 1960s, when civil liberties were on the rise in the United States. **La Raza** became a phrase utilized by Chicanos during this time to "connote pride in a pluralistic Spanish, Indian, and Mexican heritage"(Schaefer, 1988, p. 286). The term "Chicano" often carries with it strong political connotations. Not all Americans of Mexican descent wish to be called Chicanos. Some prefer to be called Mexican-American, some Mexican, and others prefer Hispanic or Latino.

Mexican History and Migration Patterns

Most Mexicans are a mix of Spanish and Indian descent and can trace their heritage back to Indian groups that built the civilizations in Mexico before the Spanish explorers arrived there in the 1500s. These Spaniards took Mexico's riches and kept the Indians poor. Often, the Roman Catholic priests from Spain taught Catholicism to the Indians, who combined it with their own religions. This special brand of Catholicism seen in today's Mexicans and Mexican-Americans is a remnant of this combination. Some of the Indian domestic arts and child-rearing practices were preserved, as the Spaniards often married Indian women. Some of the pure Indian practices, such as sorcery, witchcraft, and ancient herbal lore, still exist, but it is frequently more difficult to separate Spanish and Indian heritage in Mexicans today. Two Mexican family rules can be traced to Spanish tradition and to Mayan tradition: the idea that family honor is related to the daughter's virtue is very much a Spanish tradition; and the privileged position of the oldest son can be traced to Mayan culture (McGoldrick, eds., 1982, p. 134-135).

Some suggest that Mexicans who migrate to the United States bring with them the **oppressed servant mentality** created by the foreign domination over Mexico throughout its history. As Mexico is unsuitable for agriculture, industry, and technology, unemployment is high in Mexico. Mexicans often migrate to America with the hope of economic opportunities, and they often seem content to earn much less than the average American. Since more than one-third of the people in Mexico live in total poverty, despite working very hard, it is easy to understand their desire to migrate to the United States where they can earn more money and have a better standard of living. However, their migration to the United States is often met with negative attitudes. Due to discrimination and injustice, many Mexicans have lost their private property and rights in the southwestern area of the United States. And because they often hold illegal immigration status, it is easy for employers to take advantage of them. Many of these workers earn minimum wage and do not receive benefits such as sick pay, vacation pay, or medical insurance. It is not uncommon for several families to have to live together under one roof to cover basic living expenses. This group of people seems to have a history of being used by American businesses when it is in the corporate leader's best interests (such as the Los Braceros program); then they are dismissed when they are no longer judged to be useful (such as on-going illegal immigrant crackdowns) (Schaefer, 1988, p. 300-301).

Los Braceros Program

After World War II, the United States and Mexico agreed to the **Los Braceros program** that allowed migration across the border by contracted laborers, or braceros. More than 80,000 Mexican immigrants came to work on the Pacific Coast, often replacing Anglos in skilled trades. Throughout the 1940s and 1950s, a growing hatred of Chicanos grew, especially in relation to youths. Tension about the so-called *zoot*-**suiters** grew, and many perceived Chicanos as violent (Schaefer, 1988, p. 301-301).

Operation Wetback

To deal with the growing perceived Mexican problem, the government created the **Operation Wetback** program to round up illegal immigrants, often referred to as "wetbacks," or **mojados.** This process created an emotional climate among this population of fear of detection, social alienation, and cultural dissonance. Although this program was formally phased out by 1956, various states continue to round up immigrants who attempt to flee into the United States illegally. In the 1990s, California passed an initiative that disallowed illegal Mexicans from receiving any governmental benefits, including education, social services, and medical health. Many people think that Mexicans abuse the welfare system, when, in fact, Mexican-born immigrants rarely use welfare. They are afraid to be involved with the government for fear of being sent back to Mexico. They also see the use of welfare as negative acculturation; that is, it goes against their strong work ethic.

As was seen in Chapter 1, the Mexican population is growing and is predicted to grow even more as we move into the twenty-first century. It has been predicted that by the year 2020, the Hispanic elderly will increase 300% to about 4.8 million (Lambrinos, J. 2006). While some Americans would like to keep Mexicans out of America, that is not likely, since they are already here. Once a child is born on American land, that child is considered a legal United States citizen and is entitled to all the benefits of being American, despite his or her parent's immigrant status. Although these children were not born in Mexico, they still possess many of the cultural traditions of their parents and grandparents, and we will see these traditions as human service workers. To avoid discriminatory practices, it is vital to acknowledge that their heritage influences their current lives. Human service workers must abandon their own prejudices and hidden racist feelings. It is important to talk about ones feelings on this matter openly.

QUESTIONS FOR DISCUSSION

- In a small group, discuss your feelings about illegal immigrants.
- How do you feel about illegal immigrants receiving financial assistance and other social services?
- Do you think illegal immigrants should work in the United States?
- How do you feel about several families living in one home?
- What stereotypes and prejudices do you hold about immigrants?

Cultural Traditions in Mexican and Mexican-American Families

Most Mexican and Mexican-American families today are poor and working class, although one or two children of these families may go to college. True, there are some Mexican-Americans who are considered middle class or upper class and who work in management and professional jobs. These are the exceptions, however. More often, these families utilize their natural extended family systems for financial and emotional support. This section refers to the more-typical poor, working-class families.

Familism

Mexican-American culture values a pride and closeness amongst the family, which is often the primary source of both social interaction and caregiving (Schaefer, 1988, p. 315). The family network includes extended family, such as cousins, as well as **compadres** (close friends of the family, often from the same town in Mexico). This reliance on family and a very exclusive circle of friends can have both positive and negative consequences. On the one hand, there is much emotional support in times of family crisis, and close family support is good for the well being of the elderly. On the other hand, this family closeness can be stressful to younger generations who have become acculturated to mainstream American values and the idea of independence. This difference in acculturation often leads to depression and anxiety in the family. For example, teenagers might be discouraged from taking advantage of opportunities to attend college or accepting work outside the family because it is perceived as disloyal to the family.

CASE EXAMPLE: A 16-year-old Mexican-American girl brings home a report card to her parents. She has received excellent marks. Instead of her parents showing pride and joy, the father says, "Now, don't be thinking you're better than the rest of us. Just because you get good grades doesn't mean you are anything." This client reports that her sister, who brought home Ds and Fs, was told, "Oh well, you're just girl; you can just quit school and marry someone."

Of course, not all families respond like this. The discouragement may be in the form of **guilting** the child into loyalty and obligation to the family. An example of this might be when a college student tells her family she can't visit her grandmother because she has to study for finals and her mother responds by saying, "Too bad that you will be the only child not to visit her grandmother this vacation. I can see that your school is so much more important than your family."

Counselors must keep in mind the value of familism or familismo when dealing with Mexican and Mexican-American family issues. In these families, socialization patterns include a high degree of family cohesion and hierarchical organization. Loyalty is maintained through cooperation and affiliation rather than competition and confrontation. The family protects the individuals in the family, and it is normal for these families to live in close proximity to one another and avoid people outside the family. In return, respect for parental authority is expected throughout an individual's lifetime. Autonomy and individual achievement are not emphasized; instead, honesty and hard work are valued (McGoldrick, et al., Eds., 1982, p. 138). Large family size makes it easy to rely on the family for social interaction. Mainstream theories about family structure might refer to this type of family structure as enmeshed (very few boundaries between generations and a lack of privacy and individuality). Not only do adults live in close proximity with their family of origin, but they often live with their in-laws once they marry. This often leads to much unexpressed resentment and conflict. But, due to financial needs, sharing a residence with in-laws is often a necessity. Mother-in-laws and daughter-in-laws must learn to successfully work out these situations in order to preserve the new marriage (McGoldrick, et al., 1982, p. 139).

The culturally sensitive counselor and social worker should take into consideration the normalcy of this family structure when developing any treatment or case plan for Mexican or Mexican-American clients. Human service workers must modify their approach when dealing with this population to ensure that these deep-seated values do not get crushed. It is insensitive to force mainstream values, such as individual achievement, on this population.

Because Mexican-Americans often spend much of their lives with their family of origin, there is often a high level of emotional display in these families. When an individual spends a great amount of time with the family, emotions can run high. Human service workers must accept without judgment the dramatic tone and intense emotional expression often seen when working with Mexican-Americans.

Machismo and Marianismo

Mexican males have been heavily influenced by the Spaniard tradition of male pride and role of protector of females, often referred to as chauvinism. "This sense of virility, of personal worth in one's own eyes and in those of peers, is called machismo"(Schaefer, 1988, p. 314). This machismo does not mean that Mexican homes are male dominated, however. While the male is permitted to be aggressive and sexually experienced, it is often the mother who holds the undercover power in the family.

The Mexican woman is often described as being submissive and devoted to her children and home. This centrality of the self-sacrificing, powerful mother is referred to as marianismo. The term "marianismo" refers to the qualities found in the revered "Virgin Mary," who is strongly emphasized in the Catholic religion. These qualities of humility and virtuosity, which the Latina female endeavors to achieve, allow the male to feel his machismo; so this pairing of machismo and marianismo appears to be an effective complementary relationship. This may be a social fiction though, as the husbands are often very emotionally dependent on their wives for major decisions (McGoldrick, et al., Eds., 1982, p. 139).

Gil & Vazques (1996) describe the ten commandements of marianismo below:

1. Do not forget a woman's place.
2. Do not forsake tradition.
3. Do not be single, self-supporting, or independent-minded.

4. Do not put your own needs first.
5. Do not wish for more in life than being a housewife.
6. Do not forget that sex is for making babies—not for pleasure.
7. Do not be unhappy with your man or criticize him for infidelity, gambling, verbal and physical abuse, alcohol or drug abuse.
8. Do not ask for help.
9. Do not discuss personal problems outside the home.
10. Do not change those things which make you unhappy that you can realistically change.

The Marital and Parent-Child Subsystems

The divorce rate among Mexicans is low, partly due to religious beliefs and partly due to the focus on children as validating the marriage. Often, the relationship between parents and children is more important than the marital relationship. Romance is secondary to preservation of the marriage. Often these marriages appear to have a formal structure to them and are based on respect. No deep intimacy or intense conflict is expected, and curtailment of anger is valued. When conflict does happen, it may be a sign of different rates of acculturation between the husband and wife.

CASE EXAMPLE: A husband drinks beer on the weekends. One Saturday, the wife complains about his drinking and says that he hasn't helped with the kids. She says she is tired. He tells her to shut up and pushes her and hits her. She fights back and tells him to leave her alone.

A conflict like this may occur because the wife has asserted herself and rejected her husband's behavior. Instead of being submissive, she expressed her anger openly. This may have been learned by watching television or by listening to more acculturated women talking at the laundry mat.

In a typical Mexican family, the father is seen as the disciplinarian, while the mother provides the nurturance and support. In any case, the children are raised to show respeto (an unquestioned respect and obedience) to both parents. This respect is characterized by a dutiness and emotional dependence in which children's needs are met, but speaking up and expressing differences with their parents is not allowed.

Often, the father does not have much direct contact with the children, which strengthens the mother's role as the central figure in the family. She may do things behind the father's back for her children because she cannot openly disagree with his mandates. The mother may often feel stressed by the children and describe suffering from **los nervios** (a general state of anxiety and depression) rather than admit to feeling angry or resentful toward her children.

Because of large family size, children often play with their siblings and cousins. In comparison to American children, Mexican children have very little interaction with friends outside the family. Attending schoolmates' birthdays or slumber parties is not frequently permitted.

PUERTO RICANS

People of Puerto Rican descent hold an ambiguous status in regard to U.S. citizenship and acculturation. Christopher Columbus discovered the island in 1493, and it was under Spanish rule for four centuries, until the United States seized it in 1898 during the Spanish-American War and Spain relinquished control of it in the Treaty of Paris. The value of the island for the United States was its location, which was advantageous for maritime trade. The Jones Act of 1917 granted American citizenship to Puerto Ricans, however, the island remained a colony rather than a state. Citizens may vote for the governor of the island but may not vote for U.S. congressional representatives or president.

Despite attempts to become independent, Puerto Rico has not been allowed autonomy by the United States. Residents of Puerto Rico may come and go to the United States without any legal restrictions; however, this does not mean they may move to the mainland without challenges. Because other Latinos often attempt to pose as Puerto Ricans, their papers are scrutinized closely by immigration.

Most Puerto Ricans migrated to the U.S. mainland after World War II in the hope of finding better education and economic opportunities. Approximately 9%, or 1.2 million, of the Hispanics residing in the United States are Puerto Ricans. About 63.9% of Puerto Ricans live in the northeastern states, and about 60% live in central cities within a metropolitan area. In 1950, 81.6% of Puerto Ricans resided in New York City, whereas by 1980, only 42.7% lived there; during the economic recession of the 1970s, many Puerto Ricans returned to Puerto Rico. Despite their previous status as island residents, these returning Puerto Ricans were met with some hostility on the island, possibly due to the advanced formal schooling they received while on the mainland and the competitive edge they now had over islanders. The returning Puerto Ricans were referred to as **Neoricans** (Schaefer, 1988, p. 327-329), a derogatory term used to identify them as mainlanders who had returned.

In the Hispanic community about 8.1% of Puerto Ricans are unemployed, and they are considered to be the poorest Hispanic group. Of those living in the United States, approximately 50% of Puerto Ricans are unemployed; about 26% of Puerto Ricans live below the poverty level.

Puerto Ricans have been said to have great resiliency (Delgado, M., 1998). Delgado says this **resiliency** is due to strong coping abilities, natural support systems, social competence, and cultural pride. **Natural support systems** refers to a constellation of individuals who relate to someone on a familiar/intimate basis. They are the basis for self-definition and identity formation and meet both expressive and instrumental needs. Expressive needs are emotional needs, and instrumental needs are problem-solving needs and task guidance. Puerto Ricans living in the United States have created natural support systems in their communities that allow for the maintenance of cultural identity through the use of the Spanish language and the practice of Puerto Rican traditions. In these communities, merchants, beauty salons, small diners, laundry mats, and churches often play a pivotal role in providing expressive and instrumental needs. Delgado (1998, p. 18), discusses a study conducted by New Bridges in which various establishments in the Puerto Rican community in Holyoke, MA, were interviewed about the type of expressive and instrumental support they provided to people in need. The results showed that 18 establishments said "that people were welcome to come in to converse and not have to purchase goods or services in order to do so, 6 places provided information on social services and made referrals to social services agencies, and several establishments indicated that they provided crisis counseling, food for the hungry, loans, credit, and one place even provided child care services." Trust is essential in accepting help, and the employees working in these establishments often are trusted because they are Latino and understand the culture and the language.

The Role of Religion

While Puerto Ricans have a strong sense of cultural pride that often reflects in high self-esteem, religion does not appear to be as big an influence on this Hispanic group as it is on Mexicans. Although about four-fifths of Puerto Ricans are Roman Catholic (due to the Spanish influence), there are many who are practicing Protestants. Many choose more fundamentalist churches in which the family is supported while they adjust to life in the United States. Puerto Ricans often choose churches located in the community, creating easier access for those who do not drive.

Often, people of different ethnic backgrounds run the churches to which Puerto Ricans belong in the United States (Schaefer, 1988, p. 336-337). Yet, despite the fact that many of these clergy are of different Latino backgrounds, the Spanish language allows for maintenance of cultural identity in these houses of worship. Also, these churches are often run by ministers from the same **social economic status** (SES) as the congregation, minimizing social distance. The personality of the religious leader is very important, and this supersedes the need for him to be Puerto Rican (Delgado, M. 1998). Overall, the church provides a natural support system for this population, which is often reluctant to utilize governmental support systems (such as welfare, mental health, and other human services).

Some Puerto Ricans have been heavily influenced by African forces that incorporate metaphysical **spiritism** into their religion. This practice, Santeria, is more common among the lower-, less-educated class and is considered evil by many Puerto Ricans. The elderly populations residing in older urban areas often visit the **botanicas** (botanical shops) where products and services with significant cultural meaning and history are sold and where Santeria is understood. These shops provide medical relief, a social forum, and religious guidance. This elderly population trusts the folk healers who provide the counseling and various herbs and potions. The personal qualities of honesty and knowledge about Puerto Rican traditions engender much **confianza** (confidence) in these folk healers, and some prefer these services to Americanized medical professionals.

CUBANS

There are about 10 million Cubans living in the United States, which is 4% of the population. Two-thirds of the Cuban population lives in Florida, and it is believed that 80% live in the south. Cubans are the oldest Hispanic group living in the United States. Despite their seeming acculturation, Cubans have maintained a special identity that is based on a blending of Spanish and African cultural patterns. The lack of Indian influence has separated Cubans from other Hispanics, and has often led to racism among Latinos.

The migration pattern of Cubans to the United States has been varied and can be seen as a three-stage process. In the late 1950s, after Fidel Castro took over as dictator in Cuba, nearly 850,000 Cubans migrated to the United States to flee from communist rule. Initially, these immigrants were welcomed because they were seen as escaping the treacherous rule of communism. Since the U.S. was, at that point, in the middle of the Cold War with the Soviet Union, many so-called dissidents were welcomed as evidence that communistic rule was bad. They were seen as political refugees with whom the American public could relate and even support. Many of the first Cuban immigrants were middle- and upper-class citizens who valued education and demonstrated business sophistication. There were few racial barriers for these Cubans because many were more European in appearance (looked more "White") and they had financial backing from businesses in the United States. Many of these immigrants shared mainstream American cultural values, and a pattern of **decubanization** could be noticed among them. Some even avoided speaking Spanish and valued complete assimilation into mainstream America (McGoldrick, et al., 1982).

The second wave of Cuban immigrants came during the 1960s and 1970s in search of better education and economic conditions. This group of immigrants also held many American values. Because they lived under Castro's rule, they brought with them a unique view of the world. The powerful nation of the Soviet Union shaped their perspective and reinforced a sense of being "special" and unlike third-world Latinos.

The most recent Cuban immigrants came in the 1980s when Castro exiled many criminals and political refugees. Many of these immigrants arrived in Miami, Florida, on boats. They had no money, few work skills, a lack of education, and a history of criminal activity. These Cubans created fully operational communities in Miami that maintained strong Cuban traditions and the Spanish language.

Religion

Although Spanish Catholicism is the primary religion of Cubans, there are other religious practices, as well. Certain sectors of the Cuban population practice folk healing. This is a combination of Spanish Catholic medical and religious practices and African practices. Santeria is one such practice in which **Santeros** and **espiritistas** serve as counselors and healers who help clients by exorcizing spirits that cause illness. In Cuba this religious practice is known as **lucumi.** With families who practice Santeria, the human service worker may be able to utilize these espiritistas as a resource (McGoldrick, et al., 1982, p. 192).

Cubans who were raised under Castro's communist regime might lack a strong religious structure and may even be atheists. Often, religion was not allowed during turbulent political times when allegiance was to be given to the Communist Party.

Values

Studies of Cuban families show that Cubans value a present-time orientation and a highly active lifestyle. Also, the concept of personalismo, previously discussed, is highly valued. Cubans value people over concepts and ideas. Human service workers must consider these values when providing service. It is important to discuss a client's values with him or her. For example, some Cuban families tend to emphasize education, and for these people, it might be more beneficial to provide information than it is to provide assignments.

Family

As with most Hispanics, Cubans value a strict hierarchy in the family. The man must be the provider, and if he isn't, he loses face, self-esteem, and respeto de la familia (respect of the family). Loss of a male's self-esteem can also lead to marital and intergeneration difficulties. Familism, that is, focus on the family as the most important social unit, certainly applies to Cubans. Loyalty and unity is expected in Cuban families.

While the man's role is prescribed as machismo, the female's role is expected to be one of purity and marital fidelity. This tradition, brought by the Spaniards, often creates an asymmetrical and oppressive marital arrangement. The male is expected to have dominance and authority, while the female is expected to be submissive to her husband. This focus on female purity often leads to the **Madonna/whore syndrome**, in which the female feels guilt and shame if she enjoys her sexuality. The male also experiences difficulty in enjoying sex with his wife, because she becomes a whore in his eyes if she experiences too much pleasure.

Other Characteristics

Cubans have also been known for their **Choteo**, an exaggerated self-criticism and ridiculing of people, situations, and things. This can be a charming quality that might serve as a useful defense mechanism during times of emotional difficulties. Cubans also tend to be more informal when addressing others, often using **tu,** (informal address), versus **Usted** (more formal address). This is part of the strong personalismo noted in this culture. Some may find this choteo, or the **tuteo,** as intrusive and dramatic, but it is just the nature of the culture.

Another quality that may be taken negatively is the sense of specialness that Cubans feel as compared to other Hispanics. Since they were part of a powerful nation, Cubans often don't associate themselves with Mexicans and other third-world nationals. Some may view this attitude as arrogant; however, human service workers should always keep in mind the history of the Hispanic group with which they are working. One last quality that often differentiates Cubans from other Hispanics is their high rate and volume of speech. This may be offensive to other Spanish-speaking individuals and might even sound like a different language to some.

GLOSSARY OF TERMS

Botanicas: specialized shops in which people may purchase potions and herbs and receive spiritual advice.

Chicanos: a term used particularly in the 1960s to refer to Mexican-Americans.

Choteo: an exaggerated self-criticism and ridiculing of people, situations and things.

Compadres: a Spanish word that means a very close friend or relative who often serves as a godparent.

Confianza: a Spanish word that means trust.

Decubanization: a pattern of Cuban-identity abandonment by Cubans who immigrated to the U.S.

Espiritistas: healers and counselors who help clients by releasing evil spirits.

Guilting: a form of emotional discouragement used by Mexican-American parents to retain closeness and loyalty in their children.

Hispanos: colonized natives of the fifteenth and sixteenth centuries residing in Central and South America.

La Raza: a term used during the political movement of the 1960s to denote pride in the Mexican race.

Los Braceros: a program funded by the United States government after World War II in which Mexican laborers were contracted to work on the Pacific Coast.

Los Nervios: a mental disorder common to Latinos that is experienced as general anxiety, depression, and physical discomfort.

Lucumi: a Cuban religion in which evil spirits are exorcized.

Madonna/Whore Syndrome: a syndrome wherein a woman feels guilt and shame if she enjoys her sexuality.

Mojados: the Spanish term for "wetback," a derogatory term used to refer to illegal immigrants, because they often crossed rivers to immigrate to the United States.

Natural Support Systems: a group of individuals and groups that provide emotional and financial support to someone.

Neoricans: a derogatory term used to identify Puerto Ricans who gained an education in the United States and then returned to the island to live.

Operation Wetback: a government program designed to send back many of the illegal immigrants from Mexico.

Oppressed Servant Mentality: an attitude of helplessness about improving one's economic conditions and social status that is often found in immigrant Mexicans.

Resiliency: strong coping abilities, social competence, and ability to use resources.

Santeros: healers who exorcize evil spirits.

Social Economic Status (SES): a term used to define a group of people of the same social or economic class.

Spiritism: a primitive religion in which metaphysical concepts are believed and various aspects of nature are worshipped.

Tu: informal address

Tuteo: informally addressing someone in Spanish.

Usted: formally addressing someone in Spanish.

Zoot-suiters: a term used to describe the Mexican-American youth of the 1940s and 1950s who dressed in certain attire and who were often perceived as violent.

REFERENCES

Delgado, M. (1998). *Social Services in Latino Communities: Research and Strategies.* New York: The Hayworth Press, Inc.

Gil, J. R. M., & Vazquez, C. I. (1996). The Maria Paradox: *How Latinas Can Merge Old World Traditions with New World Self-Esteem.* New York: G. P. Putnam's Sons.

Lambrinos, J. (2006). Serving Our Hispanic Elders. Presentation given at the Human Services Conference on Poverty and Aging in Fullerton, CA.

McGoldrick, M., Pearce, J. K., & Gordana, J. (1982). *Ethnicity and family therapy.* New York: Guilford Press.

Schaefer, R. T. (1988). *Racial and Ethnic Groups, 3rd Ed.* Illinois: Scott, Foresman and Company.

CHAPTER 3

Mental Health Delivery to Latinos

INTRODUCTION

Traditional mental health services are based on a variety of theories, mostly developed by European/American clinicians. Much has been written in the professional literature regarding the need to assess whether these traditional theories are applicable to Hispanics. While many have discussed this issue, there is a dearth of actual research studies that support the hypotheses that Latinos need different mental health approaches. One reason for sparce studies dealing with the mental health treatment of Latinos is the existence of barriers in the recruitment of Latinos for psychotherapy research (Miranda, Azocar, Organista, Munos, & Lierberman, 1996). Culturally sensitive approaches that incorporate families and especially older men must be provided to recruit and retain Latinos in such research. Respect (respeto) to traditional Latino culture and warm and personal (personalismo) interactions with others must also be utilized if research with this population is to be conducted.

Most of the theories and techniques in the counseling profession were developed within a European value system. The three major camps that have traditionally defined the etiology of mental health and emotional dysfunctions can be categorized as **Behavioral, Psychoanalytic,** or **Humanistic**. If a counselor depends on these traditional theories when working with Hispanics, he or she may encounter much resistance. Table 3.1 presents traditional mainstream values as related to these traditional models and the possible Hispanic resistance to them.

Table 3.1 Comparison of Mainstream and Hispanic Values in Mental Health.

MAINSTREAM THEORETICAL MODEL	HISPANIC RESISTANCE
Behavioral Approaches to Parenting *Behavior Modification*	
a. positive reinforcement/rewards	Respeto: Children should do what their parents tell them to do, without questioning.
b. response cost/taking away privileges, restriction	Punishment is regarded as love and a way to avoid being spoiled.
c. active parenting approach	Indirect, guilt-induced methods are common with teens; parenting is not active, but assumed.
d. plan for future parenting	Deal with parenting when it comes—present orientation.
Psychoanalytic Approaches *Stages of Development Move From Complete Dependence to Complete Independence*	
a. Complete dependence	Complete dependence lasts as long as possible.
b. First independence, mobility, language, bowel control	Physically: keep on bottle or nurse sometimes up until 5 years old; hand-feed preschoolers.
c. Social independence	Socially: very few friends outside the home; plays with cousins and siblings; no sleepovers; intrafamilial dependence.
d. Moral independence	Morally: law and order; do what authority says; discouraged from making decisions on own.
e. Emotional independence	Emotionally: interdependence with parents; enmeshed boundaries; child expected to meet parents' needs.
Humanistic and Existential Approaches	
a. Self-awareness	Denial of relational conflicts; anxiety with self-awareness.
b. Confrontation of relational conflicts	Avoidance of confrontations.
c. Genuine encounters with intimacy	Lack of intimacy and authentic relating; interactions are prescribed and based on hierarchy and gender roles.

Although it may be true that these traditional mental health theories and treatment approaches are not the most effective when working with Latinos, there are a variety of approaches that are effective. We turn to understanding which types of counseling methods work best with Latinos, especially those who are the most unacculturated to mainstream American culture.

KANEL'S 2000 RESEARCH STUDY: MENTAL HEALTH OF LATINOS

To more accurately understand what Latinos believed would be useful mental health approaches, the author and several student assistants executed a research project in which approximately 300 Hispanics were surveyed about their mental health needs.

The author developed a questionnaire, which was offered in both English and Spanish to each Latino participant. This was done for several reasons. First, it was hypothesized that the majority of participants would not be able to read English and, therefore, would not be able to answer questions without an interpreter. Second, it has been recommended that translations of instruments must be conducted to achieve or approximate equivalence of meaning between the languages involved in the research (Bernal et al., 1995, p. 72) and to reduce cultural errors (Kanel, 2000b). Questions were brief and only required that the respondent circle the best response. It was hoped that the simplicity of the questions would increase completion of the questionnaire.

In addition to surveying Latinos, 43 therapists who work with Spanish-speaking families responded to a different questionnaire. Although most of the questions were multiple choice, there were a few that allowed the therapists to write in their own responses (e.g., "How do your interventions with Spanish-speaking clients differ from your interventions with other clients?") This survey was also created to be simple in the hope of increasing completion by therapists. As a result, all therapists completed it.

These surveys were distributed and collected during the 1999/2000 academic year throughout Southern California, an area with a large Hispanic population. The survey included questions related to issues facing this population and the types of interventions perceived as useful. The results of this study provide some valuable information about how mental health providers can best treat this population. The theories mentioned previously are not completely useless with Latinos, but instead may need to be modified to more appropriately treat the mental health concerns of this population. For the beginning counselor, the responses can serve as a guide to interventions that are deemed useful with Hispanics. The actual survey can be reviewed in Appendix A.

Design and Procedures

The questionnaires were distributed to the participants over a two-month period. Five student assistants participated in questionnaire distribution and collection. To obtain responses from therapists who treat Spanish-speaking clients, clinicians employed at non-profit agencies and public mental health agencies, as well as some private practice clinicians, were contacted and surveyed. The research assistants arranged to return to the agencies to collect completed surveys. The research assistants were able to find 43 therapists, approximately one to two per agency, that regularly treated Spanish-speaking clients.

The questionnaires were distributed to the Hispanic respondents in several ways. Some were distributed at a factory by a coworker. Others were distributed at laundry mats, restaurants, a produce farm, and to people residing in a neighborhood where the student assistant knew some families. Some were distributed at two local colleges, where Hispanic students in four different classes completed the surveys.

All respondents were given a brief explanation about the purpose of the research; they were told in an informed consent letter that their participation was voluntary and that they did not have to answer any questions if they did not want to for any reason. Despite this permission, most respondents answered all the questions.

After the questionnaires were collected, they were sorted into three groups: 1) the low-skilled, working-poor, Spanish-speaking group, 2) the Hispanic college students, and 3) the therapists. Following are two tables that show the demographics of the groups.

Data Analysis

In addition to tabulating frequency of responses for each group independently, frequency of responses was also tabulated for these two groups as one combined group.

A comparison between the community sample and the college sample resulted in significant findings on several variables. Not surprisingly, primary language, country of birth, and other demographic variables were significantly different between groups at the $p < .05$. Three other significant findings were found related

Table 3.2 Demographics of the Latino Participants.

	LOW-SKILLED, WORKING-POOR LATINOS (n=163)	LATINO COLLEGE STUDENTS (n=105)
PRIMARY LANGUAGE		
Spanish	88	48
English	8	48
Other	4	1
LANGUAGE SPOKEN MOST AT HOME		
Spanish	73	48
English	9	31
Both equally	12	20
COUNTRY OF BIRTH		
Mexico	73	18
United States	13	78
Other	12	4
AGE		
18-25	30	73
26-35	36	16
36-45	19	3
46-55	7	6
56-65	3	2
MARITAL STATUS		
Married	54	13
Single	31	80
Divorced	6	5
Living with other	4	2
YEARS LIVING IN THE UNITED STATES		
1-3	14	0
4-7	15	1
8-10	24	1
11-15	22	9
More than 15	23	88
LEVEL OF SPEAKING ENGLISH		
Bad	33	4
So-so	44	6
Good	20	89

Table 3.3 Demographics of the Therapist Participants.

THERAPIST GROUP	(n=43)
PERCENTAGE	
ETHNIC BACKGROUND	
Hispanic	49
Caucasian	40
Asian	5
Other	7
HIGHEST EDUCATIONAL DEGREE	
Ph.D.	12
M.S./M.S.	74
B.S./B.A.	12
No formal degree	2
LICENSE OR CERTIFICATE HELD	
Psychologist	5
LMFT (Licensed Marital and Family Therapist)	16
LCSW (Licensed Clinical Social Worker)	12
Psychiatrist	2
Other (none, intern, psychiatric technician)	56*
LANGUAGE AND CULTURAL IDENTIFICATION	
Bilingual/Bicultural	56
Bilingual	14
Bicultural	2
Neither bilingual nor bicultural	26*
TYPE OF MENTAL HEALTH PRACTICE	
Private practice	14
Nonprofit agency	49
County mental health facility	47
NUMBER OF SPANISH-SPEAKING CLIENTS SERVED PER YEAR	
0–5	23
6–10	9
11–15	2
16–20	7
21–25	9
More than 25	44*
DO YOU CONDUCT COUNSELING IN SPANISH?	
Yes	67
No	30*
DO YOU BELIEVE THERE ARE ENOUGH SPANISH-SPEAKING COUNSELORS IN ORANGE COUNTY TO MEET THE NEEDS OF LATINOS?	
Yes	2
No	88*

to whether the person 1) would make an appointment with a psychologist, 2) would prefer to take medicine or speak with a therapist, and 3) believed there were enough Spanish-speaking therapists.

Five demographic variables were found to be correlated to questionnaire items at a significance level of p<. 05. Marital status was significantly related to whether the respondent would make an appointment with a family therapist or a psychologist and whether the respondent would prefer to talk about current or childhood problems. Language spoken the most at home was found to be significantly correlated to whether the respondent would prefer to talk about current or childhood problems, as well. Country of birth, group type, and number of children were significantly related to whether the respondent would prefer to take medicine or speak to a therapist to resolve emotional problems. Lastly, number of children was significantly related to whether the respondent believed there are enough Spanish-speaking therapists.

The therapists were also asked three closed-ended questions. When asked if their formal education adequately addressed the issues and interventions mentioned by them, they were almost evenly split, with 44.2% saying no, and 46.5% saying yes. In regard to the type of relationship that they develop with this population, the majority, 61%, stated that they prefer to be "friendly but objective." A "personal" relationship was mentioned by 19%, "highly professional" was mentioned by 14%, and no one stated that they develop an anonymous or strictly doctor-patient relationship (Kanel, 2002, p. 81).

DISCUSSION

The data from this study yielded both predictable information and some results that might not have been hypothesized based on prior theoretical models. For example, it was not surprising to see that most of the respondents, including the Hispanic subjects and the therapists, believed there are not enough Spanish-speaking therapists to meet the needs of this population in Southern California. Based on the most recent Census, one could predict that because this population is growing so rapidly, there would be a need for services in all areas that accommodate their special needs, language being one of them. Another example of data that could have been predicted based on prior literature deals with the type of relationship between therapist and client that is preferred and utilized by therapists. Falicov (1982) has suggested that Mexicans prefer the initial contact with a therapist be formal, polite, and reserved. Indeed, 50% of the participants in the present study stated that they prefer that a therapist be very professional. This does not preclude the use of personalismo in which the therapist maintains an interest in the person rather than focusing on procedures, as 22% of the participants stated they prefer the therapist to be very personal. This data supports the need for mental health providers to consider personalismo when conducting counseling sessions with Latinos. This concept of personalismo may need to be studied further to extract exactly what it refers to, but one might conjecture that it is a combination of being very personal within the context of professionalism. It would appear to include techniques in which the therapist gives advice and asks many questions, as these are the interventions that the majority of the Hispanics surveyed (36% and 27%, respectively) stated they prefer in a therapist. Considering that the majority of the therapists stated that they tend to intervene with Latinos using cognitive behavioral therapy, family counseling, psychoeducational procedures, and providing referrals to other agencies, it would appear that the stated needs of the Hispanic population match what the therapists are actually doing with this population. Those particular approaches require that the therapist give more advice and ask more questions than other types of counseling approaches (e.g., person- centered and psychoanalytical models), (Kanel, 2002, p. 86).

Based on this data, therapists who work with this population may wish to take heed to this type of counseling model when working with Spanish-speaking Hispanics. Other data yielded results not readily available in the current literature and that may seem somewhat contradictory to stereotype. For example, the author had expected that more of the subjects would be in favor of medication use to help them deal with mental health problems. The fact that 59% stated that they did not believe medicine could help them and that 77% stated that they would prefer to speak to a therapist rather than take medicine suggests that mental health providers should provide counseling adjunctively if they are considering a referral for medication. The author, who has worked extensively with this population for more than 20 years, has noticed a tendency for this client group to present with many somatic complaints and express their depression and anxiety very dramatically. Typically, when clients present symptoms in this manner, they are referred to a physician for medication management, especially in large HMO facilities. Perhaps due to expense or lack of qualified counselors, it may seem easier to medicate these symptoms rather than provide the needed counseling. The current results suggest that when this type of practice exists, clients may be receiving incompetent and culturally insensitive services.

Although a few of the Hispanics surveyed stated that they would not make an appointment to see a family therapist or psychologist, (31% and 30%, respectively), the fact that 67% and 63% said they would indicates that this population does wish to receive mental health services in which counseling is the typical intervention. In further support of the idea that medication is not the preferred intervention, the majority of participants who stated that they would not make an appointment with a therapist, stated they would rather speak to friends, family, or clergy. These participants prefer to talk about their problems. Surprisingly, only one person stated he or she would prefer to visit a botanical shop for mental health problems. Theoretical models that suggest the use of botanicas (e.g., Delgado, 1998) may need to be revised because, at least in Southern California, it does not appear that Hispanics see these shops as useful for helping them with mental health issues.

One finding had to do with the role that the Hispanic's own childhood plays in mental health services. Although 64% stated that they believe that talking about childhood would help resolve current problems, only 18% stated that they preferred to talk about their own childhood in counseling. It is possible that this population has pressing issues that need to be addressed in counseling and that talking about childhood problems detracts from the valuable time needed to deal with current family problems. There has been much written about the stress common to this population related to acculturation and poverty (Quintana,1995). It may be a luxury to spend time talking about one's childhood when one is merely trying to survive current situations. The fact that none of the therapists surveyed stated that they deal with childhood issues when working with this population supports this even further. Therapists working with this population may wish to modify their approach if childhood exploration plays heavily into their therapy models.

It would appear that talking about current problems is preferred by this population, as 66% stated this preference. The type of current problems mentioned most often had to do with family issues. Nearly 54% of the Hispanic respondents stated that typical family problems include issues with children and marriage. To further support the preference to deal with current family issues, the therapists surveyed mentioned various children and family issues 69 times as the issues presented by their Spanish-speaking clients at the initial counseling session. These included family issues related to domestic violence, parenting issues, child behavioral problems, marital discord, and divorce. These results indicate that therapists who work with Hispanic clients may need skills in family and marital counseling to meet the mental health needs of this population.

Family issues are not the only problems stated to be typical for the Hispanic participants. In regard to their own emotional problems, depression and "los nervios" were mentioned as the most typical problems. In general, this fits with the therapists' responses in that the most common presenting problem mentioned was depression. However, none of the therapists mentioned "los nervios" as a present-ing problem. It may be that for the therapists, depression and "los nervios" are equivalent in terms of psychiatric nomenclature. Also, "los nervios" is not men-tioned in the **Diagnostic and Statistical Manual IV** (American Psychiatric Association, 1994), and perhaps the clinicians did not think of problems outside the formal diagnostic nomenclature. This phenomena of "los nervios" (a type of general malaise and nervousness) and what it exactly means to Hispanics, especial-ly those who are unacculturated, is examined in Chapter 4.

It would appear that Hispanics present with family problems, depression, and general malaise frequently. These problems are not uncommon for typical mental health clients. However, therapists must be culturally sensitive when treating Hispanics, keeping in mind traditional family patterns and other stresses that influence depression and other complaints. Knowledge of traditional customs and values may increase cooperation in therapy and reduce resistance. Only three of the therapists stated that there is no difference when working with Spanish-speaking clients when compared with English-speaking clients. The most frequent differ-ences mentioned by the therapists had to do with dealing with more cultural issues and using more education remedies. This corresponds with the model of group therapy proposed by Torres-Rivera, et al., (1999) in which the psychoeducational approach focuses on encouraging group members in a comparison of Latino cul-tural beliefs with the dominant culture and discussing issues at a cognitive level rather than an intrapersonal level.

The results indicate that most Hispanics surveyed would use mental health services. Of the 268 Hispanics surveyed, only 83 stated they would not make an appointment with a family therapist, and only 79 said they would not make an appointment with a psychologist. In addition, it is probable, based on the respons-es, that those who stated they would not seek out a professional to deal with their problems would seek out help from natural support systems. Indeed, 15% stated that they prefer to talk to family, friends, or clergy for family problems and 18% stated the same for their own emotional problems. Based on this data and as pro-posed by Delgado (1998), therapists may wish to consider the utilization of these natural support systems when treating this population. These natural supports may be useful adjunctively or as referral sources upon discharge.

Others surveyed indicated that they would not seek out a mental health provider due to lack of knowledge about how to use mental health services, lack of insurance, and lack of time. This data is not surprising, as poverty levels have been described as being high for Latinos, even when they are employed (Goldsmith, 1990). Also, despite being employed, Latinos often lack medical insurance that would pay for mental health services. Lastly, even if they have insurance, therapy may be perceived as a hassle, too time consuming, and too complicated to utilize. Very few stated that they would be ashamed to go see a therapist or that only crazy people go to therapists (6 and 2, respectively). This data suggests that more information needs to be disseminated to this population about how to utilize insurance, how to contact mental health providers, and how to manage time to allow for such services. Perhaps company human resource departments could be asked to arrange orientation meetings. The author has conducted several such orientation meetings at local factories and within one month after each meeting, client referrals increased dramatically (about twenty clients called within a month from each factory). Prior to those orientation meetings, the author had no referrals, despite the fact that the clients all had medical insurance available.

There were many differences between the low-skilled, working-poor Hispanics and Hispanic college students. Not surprisingly, all of the basic demographics, such as language, country of birth, marital status, and number of children, were shown to be significantly different between groups. These differences may account for difference in responses to several questions. For example, Latino college students would be less likely to make an appointment with a psychologist than would low-skilled, working-poor Latinos. But marital status was significantly correlated with making an appointment with a psychologist and may explain this between-group difference. Perhaps being married creates a type of emotional stress that college students don't experience and they, therefore, do not feel as motivated to seek out the services of a psychologist. It may also be that college students have more natural support systems for dealing with their emotional problems, and, therefore, they may not perceive a need to see a psychologist. Indeed, 31% of the college students stated they would prefer to talk to friends or family instead of a psychologist, compared to only 9% of the low-skilled, working-poor Hispanic group.

The college students also differed from the other group in their belief about whether there were enough Spanish-speaking therapists. Although only 48% of the college students reported Spanish as their primary language, as compared with 88% of the community group, they were more likely to believe there is a need for more Spanish-speaking therapists. This might be explained by the fact that college students are more aware of the mental health system and its deficiencies, due to their greater exposure to American institutions. They may have experienced lack of Spanish-speaking services personally because they use more services generally.

The last significant difference between groups related to their preference to take medicine or speak to a therapist. Although not many of the low-skilled, working-poor group preferred medicine (10%), this was significantly higher than the percentage of college students who preferred medicine (4%). This may be related to the tradition of Mexican-born individuals seeking help from medical doctors. Country of birth and this variable were shown to be significantly different.

Conclusions of the Study

This study may be just a first step in understanding the mental health needs of Latinos. The results may only be useful for those Latinos residing in Southern California, as Latinos in other parts of the country may experience different stresses. It may be a mistake to assume that all Hispanics view mental health needs in the same way. These results may, however, be useful for clinicians who treat Hispanics who were born in Mexico or whose family of origin can be traced to Mexico.

While keeping in mind cultural concepts is important, these concepts must be approached as hypotheses and must be validated by each client before they are accepted as true for the client. These results, as well as other theoretical ideas about the special issues faced by Hispanics, may serve as a guide for clinicians, as long as the clinicians remain open to the possibility that some issues presented by Hispanic clients are due to universal processes. This need to entertain both **emic** factors (those particular to the culture) and **etic** factors (those that are universal to most cultures) increases the likelihood of true cultural sensitivity, albeit it somewhat taxing on the clinician (Lopez, et al., 1989).

This study may trigger future studies that attempt to understand the relation between marital status and mental health needs for Latinos. Also, future studies may wish to compare Hispanics with non-Hispanics in search of between-group differences. Perhaps marital status for all ethnic groups influences perceived mental health needs similarly.

Traditional therapy models may have to be modified in several ways to meet the needs of Hispanics. Training programs may also wish to include discussions about personalismo and how to create it. Hispanic clients may benefit if clinicians are better trained in how to establish this type of relationship. Clinicians may also wish to learn how to incorporate natural support systems into a client's treatment. Also, people who speak Spanish may need to be recruited as mental health providers, and mental health providers who don't speak Spanish may need to learn it. Lastly, counselors may wish to learn approaches that emphasize current life stresses and family dynamics, rather than maintaining a focus on **intrapsychic** conflicts and problems from childhood.

THE IMPACT OF CERTAIN CULTURAL PATTERNS

Mexican-American cultural patterns include certain beliefs, developmental norms, and family roles and rules. One particular Mexican ideal that may differ from American norms has to do with certain child-rearing practices. In American culture, **autonomy** is stressed; in Mexican culture, however, nurturance and obedience to authority are stressed. Mexican-American children will often appear to be delayed developmentally (e.g., a 5-year-old sitting on his mother's lap, a 3-year-old drinking out of a bottle, a 14-year-old still spending all her time with her mother), but these are well within the cultural norms. The mental health professional might erroneously assess this situation as abnormal or due to psychopathology (emotional disorder). The worker must realize that these behaviors do not necessarily mean that a family dysfunction exists, and must even tolerate these differences rather than feeling anger, contempt, or disgust when these types of cultural behaviors are exhibited. A problem only exists when a Mexican-American child does not want the same type of dependency and closeness that the parent wants, due to different rates of acculturation. Keep in mind that a large percent of the therapists surveyed stated that they deal with issues of culture with their clients.

Physical distance among Mexican-Americans is another area of cultural variation. Interpreted by American standards, Mexican-American relationships might seem overinvolved, enmeshed, or overprotective. These relationships could be misinterpreted simply because family members sit closely together or because family members assume they are to be included in an individual family member's crisis (McGoldrick, et al., 1982, p. 151). A counselor must be aware of cultural differences between mainstream culture and Latino culture in order to provide the most effective services.

Issues Related to Different Rates of Acculturation

Acculturation is the process of adapting mainstream values and traditions. When family members acculturate at different rates, crises emerge in the family, often necessitating intervention by mental health workers. These crises may manifest as parent-child problems, marital problems, or may be indirectly manifested by drug abuse and alcohol abuse.

When a family first immigrates, certain behaviors are often necessary for the family to survive, but those behaviors can later become rigid and restricting for some family members. For example, when families first immigrate, many parents depend on their children to be intermediaries with the larger culture. However, the children, being raised in a culture in which children are encouraged to separate from parents, will naturally gravitate toward separation. Allowing the children to separate from them in later years can be very difficult for some parents (McGoldrick, et al., 1982, p. 155). The child may act out this conflict at school, at home, or with peers.

Conflicts can also arise when adolescents incorporate American values that are contrary to their traditional Mexican cultural patterns. Rejection of old Mexican values may be the precipitating event for a crisis with a Mexican mother or father.

Example: A 15-year-old girl may act rebelliously by dating boys, staying out late, or dressing less than modestly. A culturally sensitive counselor may suggest that the parents take a more active role in their daughter's growing up by structuring traditional activities for her, such as a quincinera (a party to announce entrance to womanhood.) The girl's acting-out behavior can then be **reframed** as her confusion about whether she's grown up or not. With a structured ritual, everyone will more easily accept role changes; this structure should help reduce the family's distress (McGoldrick, et al., 1982, p. 156).

Another behavior that might be related to different rates of acculturation is gang membership and activity. To throw off the oppressed servant mentality sometimes observed in unacculturated Latinos, adolescents might engage in activities of power and control that are common for gangs, such as drug dealing, drug use, assault, and murder. Gang activity among Latino adolescents can be considered a sign of negative acculturation because the values accepted by gang members are in complete opposition to those of traditional Mexican culture, which encourages respeto and obedience to family and authorities.

Yet another issue related to this concept may be evidenced when spouses are at different rates of acculturation. Perhaps the woman begins to display more assertive behaviors and attempts equality. She may demand communication and fair treatment. The counselor must proceed slowly and not let his or her biases toward egalitarian marriage affect the course of counseling. Maintaining a nonjudgmental attitude toward the husband is essential to minimizing resistance. The husband must be helped to see the benefits to the family and to himself of having a wife who speaks English, can drive a car, or who works outside the home.

Using negotiation skills and finding compromises are essential for the interventionist working with dual-culture families. Remember that the parents in these families have chosen to live in the United States; this decision says something about their desire to be connected with some parts of American culture. A counselor can weave this idea with positive reframes, pointing out the opportunity afforded the family by adopting certain American behavioral norms.

Acculturative Stress

Why is it that family members acculturate at different levels? Much has been written about the stress involved in the acculturation process. Perhaps some immigrants are better able to cope with the stress involved, while others lack the coping skills. Quintana, S. (1995) suggests that the relationship between the United States and Latino immigrants is paternalistic in that Latinos are viewed as less skilled and less educated. When the immigrant first moves to the U.S., then, he or she might feel inferior from the start. Coming from an inferior position would be stressful for anyone. How does the immigrant then proceed to increase his or her sense of superiority and equality? One important factor discussed has to do with learning the English language. Learning this very difficult language is in itself extremely stressful. Imagine if you had to learn Spanish in three weeks to survive and get a job. Most students feel anxious just having to learn material in their own language. Surveys have shown that Latinos are very aware of the economic disadvantages they face in not being bilingual. Quintana suggests that counselors might help the acculturating immigrant by focusing on "cultural strengths, religiosity, strong ties with their ethnic communities, and their emphasis on personal respect and deference to authority"(p.72).

Acculturation among Mexican-Americans has been studied in relation to lifetime prevalence of DSM-III disorders (Burnam, Hough, Karno, Escobar, & Telles, 1987). Interestingly, major depression, dysthymia, phobias, and alcohol and drug dependence were more prevalent among highly acculturated Mexican-Americans. In particular, those in the sample who were born in the U.S. were more likely to suffer from disorders than immigrants. These findings might suggest that acculturation is very stressful, and it might be best for Latinos to maintain their cultural customs. Perhaps these customs have resilience and support built into them that help reduce the likelihood of psychiatric disorders. It was also suggested that the reason for high rates of drug and alcohol dependence might be due to increased access when one is more acculturated.

Level of acculturation has been shown to affect college students, as well. Although level of acculturation per say was not shown to lead to psychological distress, it did have an influence on minority status stress for Hispanic undergraduate students (Saldana, D. H., 1994, p. 116). Many Hispanic students face conflicts with nonminorities on campus, suffer from discrimination, face within-ethnic group stresses, and deal with other academic concerns related to minority status. Overall, Hispanics who are first-generation students are at greatest risk for high levels of stress, perhaps due to language difficulties and lack of family support during their college tenure. For example, it is not uncommon for Hispanic college students to miss classes due to family obligations, sometimes for weeks. The author once had a student call her voicemail the night before a final exam to say he was in Mexico. Evidently, his aunt had died and he had to drive his mother to Mexico the prior day. This obligation took precedence over his own final exam.

Ethnicity Identity Formation

How does the process of acculturation develop? How does a child shift his or her ethnic identity from Mexican to American? Developing an identity is complicated even for adolescents who need not shift ethnicity identification. Adolescents are at risk for developing a variety of mental health problems because of the normal conflicts that occur during this stage of life. Adolescents of Mexican descent are no exception; in fact, they are at more risk than their American counterparts.

What puts Mexican youth at such high risk for developing emotional and behavioral dysfunctions? According to Marcell (1994, p. 323), risk factors related to this population include living at poverty level, lacking medical insurance, living in single-parent homes, residing in female-headed households with higher rates of drinking, drug use, and risk-taking behaviors, and experiencing sexual activity onset earlier than adolescents living with both parents. Additionally, insufficient bonding, poor parent-child relationships, and deficient communication and guidance could attribute to higher rates of dysfunctional behaviors among this population.

Due to the above factors, these Mexican youths often live in high-risk urban settings that are likely to entice them to exhibit more risk-taking behaviors. Also, at-school environment and teacher attitudes may lead to school failure and dropout. Dropout rates are higher among students at segregated schools, which is often the case in communities with high prevalence of Latinos, although the segregation is not legally mandated. These are the settings where identity formation occurs.

In these environments the Mexican adolescent is continually faced with stereotyping and prejudice toward themselves and their group. At the same time, they are trying to understand who they are in the context of two sets of norms: that of their group and that of the majority population. Language barriers, being part of a less-valued minority group, socioeconomic differences, and level of acculturation based on age of immigration influence their identity formation. Lastly, their identity must be formed in light of the fact that there are different Mexican groups with which to identify, such as Mexican-American, Chicano, or Cholo (gang members or very streetwise Mexicans).

When we consider all these complicating factors, it is no surprise that Mexican adolescents are at high risk for problem behavior as they form an identity and move into adulthood. Marcell (1994) suggests that the following are problem behaviors frequently found in this population: drug and alcohol use, unsafe sexual behavior, academic dropout and poor achievement, heightened risk of violent victimization, and delinquency.

The mental health worker dealing with families in which Spanish is the dominant language must find alternatives for these adolescents. These adolescents must be guided toward developing into mature adults without resorting to high-risk behaviors. Talking about the norms of their group and the mainstream society is helpful. Encouraging more involvement from parents is helpful, as well. Many of these issues must be dealt with at macro levels, that is, through changes in society itself. Another approach is to encourage the teen to become a peer mentor for others.

Family therapy that focuses on communication and adaptation to mainstream norms will be necessary in many cases. Often, the adolescent is acculturating faster than the parents, and the behavior disorder results from frustration about developing and expressing an identity that the parents find objectionable. Parents in these situations might need to be reminded that along with the advantages of immigrating to the United States often come some negatives. For example, teens in the United States are afforded more independence and are more peer oriented than in Mexico. The counselor must encourage the parents to consider how confusing it is for their teen to see other teens doing things that they are not allowed to do. Parents must learn how to communicate with their teens about the process of identity formation and acculturation and to explain that the whole family is in an identity transition. Often, when a counselor initiates these discussions, everyone in the family can relax. Perceived negative behaviors can be reframed as normal confusion rather than disobedience. Actively discussing identity formation allows parents to be involved in their teen's life, without being controlling.

Example: A 15-year-old teen was referred for counseling because she had become increasingly belligerent at home with her parents and was doing poorly in school. Communication was almost non-existent between her and her parents. This girl wanted to hang out with her friends on Saturdays, participate in volleyball after school one day a week, and attend church group one night a week. Her parents felt that she needed to spend all her time with the family. The teen came home from school every day and babysat her four younger siblings until her parents arrived home around 6-6:30 p.m. The parents couldn't understand why this daughter was so disobedient and angry all the time.

The counseling sessions focused on all of the issues mentioned above. The counselor pointed out that this teen had been attending American schools for the last 10 years and had incorporated many American values, such as the need for independence from the family and the need for peer involvement. When it was pointed out that these were considered normal in America and that she was not rejecting her parents, the parents became more understanding. Different rates of acculturation were explored, and the counselor noted how this would eventually allow the daughter to be more economically successful than the parents (this was their reason for immigrating to the U.S. in the first place). They discussed how confusing it was for the daughter to see all her school friends engaging in activities that she couldn't enjoy. The therapist also told the parents that although the daughter should be encouraged to maintain her ethnic identity as a Mexican, she would also have to incorporate being an American in there somewhere. Eventually, the parents were persuaded to loosen up and "pay" the daughter for babysitting by giving her more freedoms. It was pointed out that this arrangement would encourage the development of a strong work ethic in the daughter, a trait that the parents valued and modeled.

PSYCHOSOCIAL STRESS, PSYCHOLOGICAL DISTRESS, AND OTHER MENTAL HEALTH NEEDS OF LATINOS

There may be some similarities in the type of psychological distress that Hispanics present in mental health offices. However, the mental health worker must also keep in mind that different Latino groups may suffer differently. In a study of 593 Hispanic immigrants, Salgado de Snyder, Cervantes, R. C., and Padilla, A. M. explored the psychological distress between various Hispanic immigrant groups. Interestingly, they found that Central Americans' stress was significantly higher than Mexicans' and suggested that sensitivity to **heterogeneity** within the Hispanic population be used (p. 441). This is not to say that certain characteristics among all the Hispanic immigrants did not manifest.

The results of the research suggest that women are more likely to suffer from affective disorders such as anxiety and depression than are the men. Several explanations given by the authors included biological susceptibility, conflict of sex role expectations, lack of adequate social support networks, and lack of control over the environment. While both men and women must deal with migration stress, immigrant women also must cope with the stressors associated with the expectations and performance of their multiple roles as mothers, wives, and employees.

In general, migration leads to stress because it involves breaking lifelong ties with family members, friends, community, and cultural patterns of behavior. Immigrants are subjected to new culture and language, and many find this traumatic, although there are some who adapt well.

McGoldrick, et al., (1982, p.147-161) refer to this stress as either situational stress patterns or dysfunctional patterns of cultural transition. They thoroughly discuss the specific issues that lead to the special mental health needs of the Mexican immigrant. Poverty in and of itself creates stress for most people. Considering the high rates of poverty among Mexican immigrants, it is no surprise that lack of material resources must be addressed when treating emotional disorders. Additionally, counselors cannot ignore the social and political aspects of being an immigrant. Racism and discrimination still exist in this country, despite laws that forbid it.

Latino immigrants also tend to lack knowledge about social resources. Mental health counselors often conduct network analysis to help the family use existing networks or build new relationships to help cope with lifelong stressors. Social isolation often leads to depression and anxiety, and any intervention aimed at lessening this isolation is helpful. Using simple explanations and solutions should be considered first, before providing complex psychological understandings.

MENTAL HEALTH SERVICE UTILIZATION BY LATINOS

It may be a stereotype that Latinos do not use mental health services. Indeed, Briones, et al., (1990) suggest that because of the tremendous life stress among Mexican-Americans, they are likely to seek help for depression. They found that ethnicity, socioeconomic status, depression, and lack of social and institutional support influenced a person's readiness for self-referral to a mental health counselor. It can be conjectured then that this population will seek help in times of emotional crises, despite a tendency toward distrust of the world outside the family and friends. The notion of a **fatalistic** outlook on life due to poverty may just be a stereotype not based on reality. The research discussed at the beginning of this chapter by the text author supports this same premise. Lower-income Hispanics do see counseling as a helpful tool in relieving their depression and anxiety, as well as family problems.

EFFECTIVE MENTAL HEALTH MODELS WITH LATINOS

Now that we accept that Hispanics will seek out mental health treatment, how should a counselor approach this population? Should counseling styles change when dealing with this population? Most researchers and clinicians who focus on mental health treatment for this population suggest that brief, problem-solving crisis intervention is most suitable. Javier (1990, p. 306) proposes that these models may be based on stereotypical judgments about economically disadvantaged minorities. He states that this population has been subjected to continued deprivations throughout life, which leads to a "culture of poverty," and that the characteristics of this culture can be explained to the client in more traditional insight therapy. These characteristics include the following:

1. Strong feelings of inferiority, helplessness, and dependency
2. A high incidence of maternal deprivation
3. Weak ego structure, confusion of sexual identity, and lack of impulse control
4. Strong present-time orientation, with little ability to defer gratification and plan for the future.
5. Being at the mercy of socioeconomic-political forces outside their control
6. Maintaining a narrow view of the world and of themselves
7. A strong sense of resignation and fatalism, belief in male superiority, and high tolerance for psychological pathology
8. Preference toward action rather than observation and awareness, and tendency toward externalization and somatization rather than introspection; and
9. A view of the world as negative, a general distrust of others, and an impaired capacity for object relations.

While some Hispanics may benefit from psychoanalytically oriented therapy, the majority simply cannot afford this long-term approach; so if it is used, it must be modified. At minimum, the therapist can listen empathically and help the client feel empowered to achieve personal goals.

The Use of the Spanish Language

As discussed in Chapter 1, language is an important variable to consider when working with this population. Language is often the carrier of the culture, according to Bernal, et al., (1995). One's native language is related to the expression of emotional experiences and needs. Kanel's (2002) research and the research conducted by the Mental Health Association (1997) indicate that both clients and therapists believe there is a need for more Spanish-speaking therapists. If possible, counselors should learn enough Spanish to understand deeper emotional expressions when working with families in which Spanish is the dominant language. Understandably, this may not be possible. When this is the case, the counselor might learn enough Spanish to create an atmosphere of trust and personalismo.

In addition to speaking Spanish, the counselor might incorporate *"Dichos,"* that is, sayings or idioms, in his or her counseling. For example, when a client arrives fairly late to an appointment, or a child performs a task late, the idiom, *"Mas vale tarde que nunca"* (better late than never) might create a sense of humor about the matter. Many of the idioms and metaphors that might be helpful will come directly from the clients themselves and can be developed by the counselor for the client.

The Use of Family Therapy Models

Crisis intervention and family models have been much more widely used when working with this population. This makes sense in light of the importance of family for Hispanics. Family therapy approaches tend to focus on the role various family members play in keeping the family together, even if, at first, the behaviors seem negative. Reframing negative behavior as an unconscious attempt to keep the family together can help lower resistance in families. Additionally, the counselor may reframe certain behaviors as negative rather than positive. For example, immigrant parents often depend on older children to serve as intermediaries with the larger society and to raise younger siblings. This can be reframed as a problem by labeling it a deviation from the family's cultural heritage, which does not support children having so much power (McGoldrick, et al., 1982, p. 147-161). In this way, the **parentified** child will be relieved of inappropriate duties, and the parents will re-engage with their younger children. The parent should be convinced that only a mother and father could really care for their children appropriately. Because this population values children, this reframe cannot be resisted.

Many have proposed that structural family therapy is well suited for working with Hispanic families. It is suggested that this approach makes use of cultural reframing, which has the result of lessening resistance in these families (Szapocznik,1978). For example, many problems demonstrated by adolescents who are acting out can be reframed as a conflict between the more-traditional Latino values and the more-contemporary American values of the host culture. In this way parent-child conflicts can be reframed as cultural conflicts rather than disrespect and disobedience.

McGoldrick, et al., (1982) suggest that this approach works especially well because it carries a more emotive and dramatic tone than the objective and rational mood typically experienced in behavior modification therapies. Family therapists often ask family members to describe their feelings and reactions. As suggested previously, the use of Spanish is helpful in this expressive process. The therapist must show interest in the people involved rather than in the counseling procedures. This increases personalismo and encourages trust. Humor and diminutives soften directness, which allows for more open disclosures. This model uses stories (cuentos) and metaphors, which also aid in reducing resistance. Demanding disclosures through direct confrontation is not necessary in this model. For example, directly confronting marital conflict should be avoided in the beginning. Instead, focusing on the parent-child dyad will allow family problems to be explored.

Lastly, the family therapy model allows for a deep empathy by the counselor regarding the family's immigration struggles, including relationships with extended family and other support systems. A large part of therapy with this population includes strengthening these natural support systems. At times, mental health issues may be reframed as tasks of migration rather than individual deficiencies or mental illness.

Culturally Inappropriate Assessment: Type I and Type II Errors

Maintaining a culturally sensitive framework when providing counseling might be easy if the counselor only had to focus on Hispanic cultural needs. However, mental health workers must realize that some problems may not be cultural issues, but universal issues. This dichotomy between the particular and the universal has been dealt with extensively in scholarly literature. In essence, the mental health counselor may be prone to two different types of errors while attempting cultural sensitivity. **Type I cultural error** assumes there is a cultural process at work, when, in fact, that is not the case; this type of error often leads to stereotyping. **Type II cultural error** occurs when the counselor does not contemplate cultural information when, in fact, it does apply to the presenting situation (Bernal, et. al.,1995, p. 72). For example, some problems between Latino parents and their children may simply be due to the parents' own emotional immaturity or other psychopathology. The counselor might make a Type I error by trying to culturalize the parents' pathology. Conversely, the counselor might not consider cultural norms, such as tendency toward enmeshment, and label the parents as pathological when, in fact, they are merely behaving in accordance to Latino cultural norms (Type II error).

Lopez, et al., (1989) suggest that culturally sensitive counseling is a process whereby cultural hypotheses are constantly tested against universal hypotheses. When a counselor first begins work with Hispanic clients, the counselor must balance cultural knowledge with traditional mainstream theories of counseling and mental health.

The Use of a Curandero

Curanderismo (folk medicine) may still be an alternative mental health treatment for some Latinos. While Kanel's 2000 research did not support that this population was interested in using curanderos, there may be some older, less-acculturated Hispanics who regularly use curanderos to help overcome emotional problems, as well as physical ailments. The curandero is trusted and knows the culture well. This alone may be enough to help people through their emotional problems. Others rely on physicians for depression and anxiety. There is great respect for therapists who are considered to be experts on human relations.

Summary of Effective Mental Health Styles

In general, when conducting counseling with Hispanics, especially those less acculturated to mainstream values, a brief, problem-solving approach should be used. The focus should be on relationships between parents and children or on other relationships (such as coworkers). Emotionality, envy, and self-sacrifice are common themes and should be discussed without forcing personal insights. The counseling should be process-oriented rather than task-oriented. Venting and complaining should be encouraged, and the counselor should use any metaphors that the client presents. The use of stories—rather than confrontations—is helpful. And, when possible, the counselor should use Spanish. The use of translators is not preferable, but is sometimes necessary. If a translator must be used, do not use the parent's own child to translate personal information.

GROUP THERAPY

Torres-Rivera, et al., (1999) discuss their group work with Latino clients. They state that their experience suggests that the socio-process (psychoeducational) group modality as developed and proposed by Betz, et al., (1981) and Wilbur, Roberts-Wilbur, and Betz (1981) is effective in working with Latinos in groups. They suggest that the nature of these groups allows for personalismo among groups members due to the focus on members' ideas, attitudes, values, and beliefs relative to specific topics or concerns of the group members. It is proposed that because a psychoeducational group is not a counseling or therapy group, members will discuss issues at a cognitive and interpersonal level rather than at an emotional or intrapersonal level (p. 393). Torres-Rivera, et al., go on to state that in their experience, topics most germane for Latino clients are developmental, familial, relational, and political-historical. Also helpful are discussions in which members compare Latino cultural beliefs with the dominant culture.

The group leader does well to listen and provide understanding rather than solve particular problems. As the members understand that some of their conflicts in life are related to differences in their cultural beliefs and attitudes from the dominant culture, they may become more self-accepting and perhaps reduce self-defeating behaviors. As with all counseling work with Latinos, counselors must maintain an open multicultural perspective and leave stereotypes and biases elsewhere.

GLOSSARY OF TERMS

Acculturation: the process of integrating mainstream values and traditions.

Autonomy: a state of independence and self-sufficiency.

Behavioral: a theory that suggests all behavior is learned and can be extinguished through removal of positive reinforcement and increased through rewards.

Curanderismo: a type of folk healing practiced by many Latinos, especially the elderly.

Diagnostic and Statistical Manual 4th Ed. (DSM): the book that mental health clinicians use to decide which label to give clients. The diagnoses are based on various behavioral criteria.

Emic: a term that refers to the particular characteristics of a culture.

Etic: a term that refers to the universal components of cultural behaviors.

Fatalistic: holding negative and pessimistic attitudes about the future.

Heterogeneity: a term that refers to the idea that even within certain cultural groups, differences exist among individual members of that group.

Humanistic: a model that focuses on self-examination and open communication to facilitate self-esteem and meet individual needs.

Intrapsychic: a psychoanalytic term that refers to hypothesized psychological features within one's mind.

Parentified: when a child plays the role of a parent.

Prejudice: the holding of preconceived feelings, usually negative, toward someone because of the cultural group to which he or she belongs.

Psychoanalytic: a model that focuses on early childhood experiences determining adult life, as well as unconscious forces that create inner conflict.

Reframing: a technique in which a counselor helps the client view the situation from a different perspective.

Respeto: the belief that children should do what their parents tell them to do, without questioning their authority.

Stereotyping: the act of attributing characteristics to someone because of the ethnicity to which she or he belongs.

Type I Cultural Error: occurs when one assumes that a cultural process is at work when, in fact, that is not the case.

Type II Cultural Error: occurs when a therapist fails to take into consideration cultural variables that may be influencing behaviors.

REFERENCES

Bernal, G., Bonillo, J., & Bellido, C. (1995). Ecological validity and cultural sensitivity for outcome research: Issues for the cultural adaptation and development of psychosocial treatments with Hispanics. *Journal of Abnormal Child Psychology, 23*, 1, 67-85.

Briones, D. F., Heller, P. L., Chalfant, H. P., Roberts, A. E., Aguirre-Hauchbaum, S. G., & Farr, W. F. (1990). Socioeconomic status, ethnicity, psychological distress, and readiness to utilize a mental health facility. *American Journal of Psychiatry, 147*, 10, 1333-1341.

Burnham, M. A., Hough, R. L., Karno, M., Escobar, J. I., & Telles, C. A. (1987). Acculturation and Lifetime Prevalence of Psychiatric Disorders Among Mexican Americans in Los Angeles. *Journal of Health and Social Behavior, 28*, 89-102.

Falicov, C. J. (1982). Mexican families. In M. McGoldrick, J. K. Pearce, & J. Giordano (Eds.), *Ethnicity and family therapy.* New York: Guilford.

Javier, R. A. (1990). The suitability of insight-oriented therapy for the Hispanic poor. *American Journal of Psychoanalysis, 50*, 4, 305-318.

Kanel, Kim. (2000b). Special challenges Japanese Learners of English Face. *The JASEC Bulletin, 9*, 1, 43.

Kanel, Kristi. (2002). Mental Health Needs of Spanish-speaking Latinos in Southern California. *Hispanic Journal of Behavioral Sciences, Vol. 24*, No. 1, 74-91.

Lopez, S. R., Grover, K. P., Holland, D., Johnson, M. J., Kain, C. D., Kanel, K., et al. (1989). Development of culturally sensitive psychotherapists. *Professional Psychology: Research and Practice, 20*, 369-376.

Marcell, A. V. (1994). Understanding ethnicity, identity formation, and risk behavior among adolescents of Mexican descent. *Journal of School Health, 64*, 8, 323-328.

Mental Health Association of Los Angeles. (1997). "Human Resource Needs Assessment: Human Services Industry." Los Angeles, CA: Author.

Miranda, J., Azocar, F., Organista, K. D., Munos, R. G., & Lieberman, A. (1996). Recruiting and retaining low-income Latinos in psychotherapy research. *Journal of Consulting and Clinical Psychology, 64,* 5, 868-874.

Quintana, S. M. (1995). Acculturative stress: Latino immigrants and the counseling profession. *The Counseling Psychologist, 23,* 1, 68.

Saldana, D. H. (1994). Acculturative stress: Minority status and distress. *Hispanic Journal of Behavioral Sciences, 16,* 2, 116-128.

Snyder, V. N., Salgado de, Cervantes, R. C., & Padilla, A. M. (1990). Gender and Ethnic Differences in Psychosocial Stress and Generalized Distress Among Hispanics. *Sex Role, 22,* 7/8, 441-453.

Szapocznick, J., Scopetta, M. A., & King, O. E. (1978). Theory and practice in matching treatment to the special characteristics and problems of Cuban immigrants. *Journal of Community Psychology, 6,* 112-122.

Torres-Rivera, E., Wilbur, M. P., Roberts-Wilbur, J., & Phan, L. (1999). Group work with Latino clients: A psychoeducational model. *Journal for Specialists in Group Work, 24,* 4, 383-404.

CHAPTER 4

Special Issues Facing Latinos in the United States

ATAQUE DE NERVIOS

Introduction

As discussed in Chapter 3, the use of metaphors by Latinos may help them cope with shameful issues by dealing with them indirectly. An example might be the very pervasive complaint referred to as **Ataque de Nervios,** only observed in Latinos. Instead of directly focusing on anger, guilt, fear, or feelings of helplessness, many Latinos, especially women, state they have been attacked by a case of nerves. This is often experienced as having been taken over by an outside force (los nervios). The client usually feels that he or she has no personal part in los nervios. Los nervios might manifest as depression, anxiety attacks, fatigue, agitation, or all of these. Descriptions of ataque de nervios resemble those of panic attacks, except that there is typically an absence of fear during the ataque, and they are more common during times of familial stress (APA, 1994). It is usually with great surprise that the client connects los nervios with psychosocial stress. Depending on the client and level of acculturation, a variety of interventions are successful in combating los nervios. Some elderly, very unacculturated women may seek the help of a curandero at a botanica (shop owner at a botanical shop). Others may seek the aid of a medical doctor, who may offer antidepressants or sleeping pills. Yet others seek the help of mental health counselors. By allowing the client to talk in a free association style, los nervios seems to dissipate over time. Direct confrontation is not recommended, but rather the counselor should maintain the metaphor of an outside force overtaking the client and let the process of relief happen without major insight.

Kanel's 2004 Study

The author (Kanel, 2004) conducted a study in which the phenomenon of Ataque de Nervios was examined. Although this syndrome has been studied, most research has focused on how Puerto Ricans have experienced Ataque de Nervios. Kanel believed it was just as important to understand how Mexican-Americans perceive this phenomenon, as they are the largest Latino group in the U.S. Kanel was particularly interested in understanding how mental health practitioners should diagnose this disorder, as it is not listed as a possible diagnostic label in the Diagnostic and Statistical Manual Fourth Edition, although it is mentioned in the appendix, which outlines cultural formulation and a glossary of culture-bound syndromes (American Psychiatric Association (APA), 1994, p.843).

While there does appear to be some understanding of this syndrome, there is also some confusion. Primarily, clinicians cannot be quite certain as to which traditional DSM-IV diagnosis they should label clients who report suffering from Ataque de Nervios. It has been associated with several anxiety disorders, affective disorders, and dissociative disorders (Koss-Chioino, 1999; Liebowitz, et al., 1994; Oquendo, 1993; Salman, et al., 1998; Schechter, et al., 2000). Uncertainty in diagnosis can have an effect on appropriate treatment approaches.

Operational Definition of Ataque de Nervios

This syndrome has been described sufficiently in the literature. It has been referred to as a self-labeled illness experienced as a panic attack, fit of violent agitation with self mutilative, and suicidal behavior by Schechter, et al. (2000, p. 530). Liebowitz, et al. (1994, p. 871) describe it as an illness category used by Puerto Ricans and other Hispanics that includes behaviors such as shaking, heart palpitations, sense of heat rising on the head, numbness of hands, shouting, swearing, striking others, falling, and convulsing. It has also been described as a seizure-like response with signs of dissociation, suicidal fits, and panic-like responses (Oquendo, 1995, p. 60).

METHOD

Participants

Two different groups of participants were surveyed. One group consisted of 198 Latinos whose dominant language was Spanish. Table 4.1 presents the demographic information on this group, including variables such as age, place of birth, education, and ethnic identification. The second group of participants consisted of 37 mental health clinicians who self-described themselves as regularly treating Spanish-speaking clients. See Table 4.2 for information regarding place of employment, cultural makeup, type of mental health practitioner, and so forth. All participants completed the surveys voluntarily and lived or worked in Southern California.

Materials

The author developed a questionnaire for the Hispanic group using back-translation and committee evaluation procedures. Each participant was offered either the English version or the Spanish version of the survey. The questionnaire consisted of basic demographic questions, several open-ended questions that asked about their own description of Ataque de Nervios, and multiple-choice questions in which the participant was asked to circle symptoms and behaviors that they thought were characteristics of Ataque de Nervios. These characteristics were taken directly from DSM-IV (APA, 1994: p. 436, for generalized anxiety disorder; p. 395, for panic attack/panic disorder; p. 327, for major depression) and were separated into three different questions so as to identify how many symptoms were being circled for the three diagnoses of major depression, panic disorder, and generalized anxiety disorder. These diagnoses were chosen because prior mental health studies seemed to indicate these diagnoses most often correlated to the self-labeled syndrome of Ataque de Nervios (Koss-Chioino, 1999; Liebowitz, et al., 1994; Oquendo, 1995; Salman, et al., 1998; Schechter, et al., 2000). Additionally, participants were asked what they thought caused Ataque de Nervios, how long it lasted, and what interventions were used to help.

Another questionnaire was developed for the therapists to complete. The questions were multiple choice and included the identical list of characteristics of Ataque de Nervios given to the Hispanics subjects, separated into three questions so as to correspond with the diagnoses of major depression, panic disorder, and generalized anxiety disorder. They were also asked about treatment approaches and perceived causes.

Design and Procedures

Prior to administration, all measures and study procedures were approved by the Institutional Review Board at California State University, Fullerton. Written informed consent forms were read and approved by all study participants. For participants who could not read, the material was read to them by research assistants.

Table 4.1 Demographic Information for the Latinos (in raw numbers)

Variable	Latino group (n=198)
AGE OF SUBJECTS	
18-25	25
25-35	77*
36-50	64*
51-62	32
GENDER OF SUBJECTS	
Males	88
Females	108*
PLACE OF BIRTH	
USA	25
Mexico	146*
Central America	13
South America	10
Cuba	1
Puerto Rico	1
Other	1
ETHNIC IDENTIFICATION	
American	4
Mexican-American	27
Latino	64
Hispanic	90*
Other	13
EDUCATION	
Less than 8 years	47
Completed high school	69
Some high school	26
College degree	17
Some college	36
MARITAL STATUS	
Married	104
Divorced	14
Separated	21
Single	54
Other (widowed)	4
YEARS LIVING IN THE U.S.	
1-5	22
6-10	27
11-15	55
16-20	26
21 or more	63
HAVE YOU EXPERIENCED OR KNOWN SOMEONE WHO HAS EXPERIENCED ATAQUE DE NERVIOS?	
Yes	138
No	60

Table 4.2 Therapist Group Demographics (in raw numbers)

Characteristic	Raw numbers (n=37)
TYPE OF LICENSE	
Licensed Marital and Family Therapist	6
Licensed Clinical Social Worker	2
Psychologist	3
Psychiatrist	1
Non-licensed Counselor	22
Other	3
PLACE OF EMPLOYMENT	
County Behavioral Health	4
Non-Profit Agency	22
Managed Care Facility	3
Private Practice	6
Residential Facility	1
Other Social Welfare Services	1
CULTURAL MAKEUP	
Bilingual	
Yes	18
No	20
Bicultural Latino and American	
Yes	15
No	22
Spanish-speaking Clients Seen Yearly	
0-5	9
6-10	4
11-15	5
16-20	1
21-25	3
25+	16*
HAVE YOU SEEN CLIENTS WITH ATAQUE DE NERVIOS?	
Yes	23
No	14
HOW MANY CASES HAVE YOU DEALT WITH?	
0-3	6
4-6	4
7-9	3
10-12	1
13+	10*
DO YOU THINK ATAQUE DE NERVIOS SHOULD BE A SEPARATE DSM DIAGNOSIS?	
Yes	11
No	12

Participants were informed that their participation was voluntary and that they did not have to answer any questions if they not want to for any reason.

The questionnaires were distributed to the Hispanic respondents in several different ways. Some were distributed at supermarkets, laundry mats, flower shops, banks, ESL classes, libraries, churches, and factories in three neighboring counties with high percentages of Latinos (Orange, Los Angeles, and San Bernardino Counties). Precedence for collecting data from community settings has been set by Delgado (1998) and Kanel (2002) and has been shown to increase participation and comfort in Latinos participating in research. To obtain responses from therapists who treat Spanish-speaking clients, clinicians who work in various mental health settings were contacted, and surveys were distributed. The assistants arranged a date and time to return to the agencies to collect completed surveys if the clinicians were not able to complete them at time of distribution. A total of 37 therapists were found who regularly treat the population of concern.

Data Analysis

In addition to tabulating frequency of responses for each group independently, correlational tests between demographic variables and whether the respondent had experienced or known someone who had experienced Ataque de Nervios were conducted. There were no significant correlations between any demographic variable and the experience of Ataque de Nervios.

The written responses to the open-ended questions were translated into English by a bilingual/bicultural research assistant and were tallied as to frequency of spontaneously written answers (see Table 4.3). If a subject answered no to "Have you experienced or known someone who has experienced Ataque de Nervios?", they were instructed not to complete the questionnaire. Only those who answered yes (n=138) to this item were tabulated for the remainder of the survey. The same held true for clinicians who answered no to "Have you seen clients with Ataque de Nervios?" The final sample of clinicians who said yes to this question was 23, and only their responses to the remainder of the survey were tabulated.

The responses to the multiple-choice items were tabulated as to frequency and percentage for both the Hispanic group and Therapist group. Because the results were so close for the Latino group, a simple T-test was used to compare means of total symptoms reported for each diagnosis. The symptoms of Panic Disorder were shown to be significantly higher (m=2.2462) than either Major Depressive episode (m=2.0077) or Generalized Anxiety Disorder (m=2.0382) at the .0001 level. In order to ascertain if an actual diagnosis would be indicated, tabulations were done to examine how many participants selected the 5 characteristics needed to make a formal diagnosis from each of the specific questions. Almost 33% of the Hispanic participants chose 5+ symptoms from the Panic Disorder question, compared to 23.1% for Major Depressive episode and 23.6% for Generalized Anxiety Disorder. In contrast, 60% of the clinicians selected 5+ symptoms from both Panic Disorder and Generalized Anxiety, and 30% selected 5+ symptoms from Major Depressive Disorder.

Because the DSM requires at least 5 symptoms to be present in order to make the diagnosis, tabulations were conducted to identify how many subjects reported 5 or more symptoms for each diagnosis. Out of the 138 subjects who said yes to having experienced or known someone who had experienced Ataque de Nervios, 37% reported fewer than 5 symptoms for any diagnosis, 39% reported 5 or more symptoms for 2 or more diagnoses, 20% reported 5 symptoms for only 1 diagnosis, and 3% reported 4 symptoms for at least 2 diagnoses. This means that 77% of respondents qualified either for no diagnosis or for 2 or more diagnoses!

Only 30% of the clinicians reported 5 or more symptoms for Major Depression, while 60% reported 5 or more symptoms for both Panic Disorder and Generalized Anxiety Disorder. Overall, the Latino group reported more symptoms for Panic Disorder than the other two disorders, while the clinicians reported equal amounts of symptoms for both Panic Disorder and Generalized Anxiety Disorder. When the clinicians were asked what formal label they typically give Ataque de Nervios, 50% reported Generalized Anxiety Disorder, 26% reported Panic Disorder, 21% reported Major Depression, and 13% reported Other. These results indicate much overlapping and confusion in diagnosis.

Other data, such as perceived causes, duration, and interventions for Ataque de Nervios as answered by both groups were tabulated independently as frequencies, as seen in Table 4.4. Family conflicts, emotional problems, and work conflicts were reported most often as causes of Ataque de Nervios by Hispanics. The clinicians reported family conflict as the number one cause, followed by intrapsychic conflict, childhood abuse, and drug and alcohol abuse.

When asked what they did to overcome Ataque de Nervios, 31% of Latinos reported that they talked to family or friends, 21% saw a therapist, 21% received medication from a primary care physician, 17% said it went away by itself, 12% received medication from a psychiatrist, 10% saw a curandero, and 14% reported other (e.g., chiropractor, prayer, hands-on healing, or smelling alcohol or onions). The types of medications ranged from antianxiety drugs to antidepressants, sleeping pills, and pain pills. The clinicians reported cognitive therapy as the most-frequent treatment approach, followed by supportive therapy, family therapy, medications, and, rarely, expressive therapy and psychoanalytic therapy (see Tables 4.5 and 4.6).

The clinicians were also asked if they thought Ataque de Nervios should be a separate diagnosis in the DSM. Of the 24 who responded to this question, 11 said yes, and 13 said no.

The Latino group was asked how long Ataque de Nervios lasted. The range was from 5 minutes to 20 years.

(Items in parentheses are exact words used by respondents. Numbers indicate how many people wrote that behavior. When more than one behavior is listed, the number in the next column applies to all in the cell.)

DISCUSSION

The results not only support much of what has been reported in previous studies, but expands the knowledge base about Ataque de Nervios to include Hispanics of Mexican descent. The fact that 138 out of 198 (70%) non-clinical participants reported having either experienced or known someone who had experienced Ataque de Nervios indicates widespread knowledge of this syndrome among Latinos, primarily of Mexican descent, residing in Southern California,.

Likewise, 23 out of the 37 (62%) clinicians surveyed reported having treated Ataque de Nervios. This expands the prior research sample of Latinos of Puerto Rican descent to include the most-predominate ethnic group in America, Latinos of Mexican descent, as well as those of Central and South American descent.

These Latinos were not completely unacculturated people, as 72% of the 198 Latinos surveyed reported living in the USA for more than 10 years. Since they reside in this country, it may be time to include their experience of Ataque de Nervios in our taxonomy, not as a culture-bound syndrome, but as a syndrome under the anxiety disorders. The syndrome is evidently seen in abundance, not just in the elderly, unacculturated Latinos who seek curanderos for folklore illnesses. It is now a syndrome observed in Americans of Latino descent who are the majority population in many places (e.g., East Los Angeles, CA, with an estimated 96.8% Latino population; Los Angeles, CA, with 47% Latino population; Santa Ana, CA, with 76% Latino population) (Becerra & Alvarez, 2001). New York City houses the most Latinos in number (2.16 million), and Latinos make up 27% of that city's total population (McDonnell, 2001).

There would be no need to even consider adding Ataque de Nervios to current nomenclature if the current labeling system adequately identified the syndrome, thereby allowing for proper treatment. As this study shows, 39% of the Latinos describe Ataque de Nervios symptoms as qualifying for more than 1 diag-

Table 4.3 Subject's Description of Ataque de Nervios in their own words (after translation) n=138

BEHAVIOR	FREQUENCY OF THOSE WHO WROTE THIS BEHAVIOR
Screaming	20*
Despair	18
Out of Control	16
Crying	15
Anxiety	14
Everything irritates you	11
Body tremors	9
Inability to sleep Can't breath Strike/hit/break something	8
Get angry Pass out/faint Lose control of emotions	7
Feeling depressed (deprimido)	5
Sleep a lot Run/walk away Hurt others or self Feeling nervous (nerviosa) Want to die	4
Feeling sad (triste) Worried (preocupado) Hands shake Fear (miedo) Scared (temor) Can't speak Something bad is going to happen	3
Loss of appetite, consciousness Want to avoid bad things Not able to perceive what is going on Annoy others Can't concentrate Talk to self Feel weak/tired	2
Weight gain Need to catch breath Suffocation Overwhelmed Can't think clearly Sweating Headaches Possessed by evil, hear voices	1

Table 4.4 Frequency of Responses Related to Observed or Experienced Characteristics of Ataque de Nervios as Categorized by 3 Diagnoses

DIAGNOSIS	LATINOS (n=138)	CLINICIANS (n=23)
Major Depressive Episode		
1-2 symptoms	45/22.6%	
3-4 symptoms	39/19.6%	16/69%
5+ symptoms (warrants diagnosis of major depressive episode)	46/23.1%	7/30%
Panic Disorder (Panic Attack)		
1-2 symptoms	33/16.6%	
3-4 symptoms	32/16.1%	9/24%
5+ symptoms (warrants diagnosis as panic disorder)	65/32.7%	14/60%
Generalized Anxiety Disorder		
1-2 symptoms	42/21.1%	
3-4 symptoms	42/21.1%	9/39%
5+ symptoms (warrants diagnosis of generalized anxiety disorder)	47/23.6%	14/60%

Table 4.5 Perceived Causes of Ataque de Nervios by Both Hispanics and Clinicians

CAUSE	HISPANICS (n=138)	CLINICIANS (n=23)
Family conflict	111/76%*****	19/82%****
Emotional problems	107/73%*****	
Work conflicts	84/58%	
Poor physical health	48/28%	
Mental illness	41/28%	
Being a bad person	13/9%	
Possession by a demon	10/7%	
Other: (curse, genetics-2 people, lack of affection, infidelity, can't express feelings, can't face something bad, envy, love problems, loss, money, car accident)	25/17%	
Biochemical imbalance		6/26%
Intrapsychic conflict		9/39%
Childhood abuse		9/39%
Immaturity		4/17%
Drugs and alcohol abuse		10/43%
Other		2/.09%

(The Hispanic group was asked to circle all perceived causes from a list of causes. The clinicians were asked an open-ended question about what they perceived the causes to be.)

Table 4.6 Latino Responses to "What was done to help overcome Ataque de Nervios?"

Talked to family and friends	45/31%
Saw a therapist	30/21%
Got medication from a PCP	30/21%
It went away by itself	25/17%
Got medication from a psychiatrist	18/12%
Saw a curandero at a botanica (spiritual cleansing, herbs and teas, exercise, psychic reading)	14/10%
Other (chiropractor, prayer, hands-on healing, smelling onions and alcohol)	21/14%

Table 4.7 Types of Treatment Approaches Used by the Clinicians

Cognitive therapy	14/60%
Supportive therapy	13/56%
Family therapy	11/48%
Medications (anxolytics, Benzodiazapeme, Paxil)	10/43%
Expressive therapy	2/.08%
Psychoanalytic therapy	2/.08%

nosis, and 37 % didn't report enough symptoms to qualify for even 1 diagnosis. According to these results then, there might be confusion in proper diagnosis for 76% of individuals who present with the complaint of Ataque de Nervios. This confusion of proper fit between Ataque de Nervios and DSM has been reported by others in their studies of this syndrome (Koss-Chionino, 1999; Oquendo, 1995; Salman, et. al, 1998; Schechter, et al, 2000). Ataque de Nervios has been studied in clinical settings to understand whether it is the same thing as traditional DSM disorders such as Panic Disorder, etc. None of these studies resulted in an exact fit with traditional diagnoses, and most recommended further study to better understand the relationhsip between Ataque de Nervios and other disorders (Koss-

Chioino, 1999; Liebowitz, et al., 1994; Oquendo, 1995; Schechter, et al., 2000).

One might argue, then, that those cases might be given a diagnosis other than Panic Disorder, Generalized Anxiety Disorder, or Major Depressive Episode (which have been the DSM diagnoses usually studied). Perhaps a catchall disorder such as Adjustment Disorder with anxious, depressed, or mixed emotional features is a better fit. But does this adequately describe what is going on? Why not call it what it is, Ataque de Nervios, and treat it as such? True cultural sensitivity does not relegate a widely known syndrome to the appendix of a medical book; it does not try to make Ataque de Nervios fit into American nomenclature. True cultural sensitivity understands and treats a cultural phenomenon from the perspective of its creators.

Ataque de Nervios is often treated with medications and sometimes adjunct cognitive/behavioral therapy. In fact, the clinicians in the current study indicated that treatment should include family therapy, supportive therapy, cognitive therapy, and medication. Yet, Panic Disorder, Generalized Anxiety Disorder, and Major Depressive Episode are rarely treated with family therapy. However, 48% of the clinicians in this study mentioned family therapy as a preferred treatment for Ataque de Nervios. Other studies (Liebowitz, et al., 1994; Oquendo, 1995) have also supported the use of family therapy, as well as supportive therapy, for Ataque de Nervios. Due to its confusion with other disorders, Ataque de Nervios may sometimes result in unnecessary hospitalization or medication (Oquendo, 1995, p. 60). In his study, Dr. Oquendo also suggests that Ataque de Nervios be recognized as a separate syndrome and not be treated with pharmacological, behavioral, or cognitive interventions specific to panic disorder (p. 62).

The participants in the current study agreed with this idea, stating that talking to family and friends is the appropriate treatment for the syndrome (31% selected this as their answer to what was done to help overcome Ataque de Nervios). It is doubtful that people with Panic Disorder, Generalized Anxiety Disorder, or Major Depressive Episode would believe talking with family or friends would help their conditions. Also, only 2 participants believed it was genetic, and only 21% received medication from a PCP and 12% from a psychiatrist. This contrasts with typical treatment for the DSM diagnoses mentioned, which almost always includes medication, as they are considered to be caused by genetic and biochemical factors.

As far as perceived causes of Ataque de Nervios, both groups overwhelmingly selected family conflicts as the primary factor for onset (76% of Latinos, 82% of the Clinicians). One wonders if clinicians would give this same response regarding causes of the DSM diagnoses referred to above. Emotional problems and work conflicts were mentioned as the next two causes by the Latino group. This indicates that the perceived causes are interpersonal stress of some sort, in combination with emotional problems. Interestingly, 43% of the clinicians perceived drugs and alcohol abuse to be at the root of Ataque de Nervios, along with childhood abuse (39%) and intrapsychic conflict (39%). One might conclude from these results, then, that Ataque de Nervios is caused from a combination of current family conflicts, childhood abuse, immature psychological development, drug and alcohol abuse, and current work conflicts. Only 26% of the clinicians stated that a biochemical imbalance was the root cause of the syndrome. This is at variance with the root causes usually given for the DSM diagnoses considered for Ataque de Nervios. Panic Disorder, Major Depressive Episode, even Bipolar Disorders, are all believed to be caused by biochemical imbalances.

CONCLUSION

Based on these results, it appears that Ataque de Nervios is a separate syndrome that should not be confused with current DSM nomenclature. It has been shown that while the symptoms may be similar to current DSM labels in some instances, they may also be different or overlapping. The perceived causes of Ataque de Nervios appear to be different than those usually assigned to DSM labels. Treatment approaches for Ataque de Nervios also differ from typical approaches used for DSM labels. Keeping in mind these differences, it may be time to give Ataque de Nervios its own label. Following, is an example of how this new diagnosis might be listed in the next DSM edition, under Anxiety Disorders.

ATAQUE DE NERVIOS

Diagnostic Features

The essential feature of Ataque de Nervios is a sense of feeling out of control, often in reaction to interpersonal stress. These feelings may take the form of screaming, crying, feeling despair, feeling anxiety, feeling dizzy, and feeling irritated. It may present with many symptoms of Panic Disorder, Generalized Anxiety Disorder, Major Depressive Disorder, Somatization Disorder, and Dissociative Disorders.

Specific Culture, Age, and Gender Features

This disorder is usually seen in Hispanic individuals. It may be more prevalent in women.

Course

People suffering from Ataque de Nervios have reported it lasting from 5 minutes to a few months. It often goes away on its own if treatment is not sought.

Diagnostic Criteria for Ataque de Nervios

A. A person of Latino descent reports suffering from Ataque de Nervios

B. There is no history of Bipolar Disorder or Panic Disorder

C. The complaints fit into one of the following subtypes:

1. **Ataque de Nervios with panic:** predominately feeling out of control, can't breath, want to hit something, screaming, needing to run away, getting angry, body tremors

2. **Ataque de Nervios depressed type:** predominately feeling sad, crying, wanting to die, inability to sleep, feeling something bad will happen, loss of appetite, hurting self, oversleeping, feeling depressed, despair

3. **Ataque de Nervios dissociative type:** fainting, loss of consciousness, can't speak

4. **Ataque de Nervios somaticized type:** pain in the body, fear of having a sickness

5. **Ataque de Nervios general type:** anxiety, hands shake, scared, worried, everything irritates them

Of course, this is just a preliminary model, but it is worth investigation by the American Psychiatric Association.

LATINO TEENAGE PREGNANCY

Teenage pregnancy among Latinas (female Latinos) is higher than in any other ethnic group. According to the Sixth Annual Report on the Conditions of Children in Orange County, CA, (Orangewood Children's Foundation & Center for Collaboration for Children, 2000), in 1998, "Hispanic females under 19 years of age accounted for 75.6% of total births to teens. Non-Hispanic white females had 18.4% of the total births to teens, followed by Asians at 3.9% and African Americans at 1.7%" (p.34). This is a 2.2% increase in births for Hispanic teens between 1994 and 1998."

This is not to suggest that Latinas engage in more sexual activity than other ethnicities. In fact, in a study by Remez (1991), it was discovered that Mexican-American adolescents born in Mexico are less likely to begin sexual activity at a young age than non-Hispanic Whites or U.S.-born Mexican-Americans. Despite this difference, however, Mexican-born adolescents still have the highest rates of early pregnancy and childbearing because they are the most likely to become pregnant once sexually active and the least likely to terminate a pregnancy.

There may be a variety of reasons why so many Hispanic girls become pregnant. One includes the fact that sexuality is rarely addressed openly in Latino families. Females are assumed to be virgins until they marry; then they are expected to reproduce as many children as God sees fit to give to them. In contrast, Hispanic males are assumed to be sexually experienced and virile. Who are the men having sex with? It would appear that the sexual relations with unmarried Latinas are kept secret in order to maintain the cultural myth Latina purity. When an unmarried Latina, usually a teenager, becomes pregnant (Latinas usually get married very young in comparison with mainstream American women), the focus is on the upcoming blessed event—the birth of a new grandchild. The fact that she was having unprotected sex is rarely talked about in the family. Another reason adolescent Latinas have higher pregnancy rates is because they marry earlier than other ethnicities. Unfortunately, this sometimes lends itself to a perpetual cycle of poverty and child abuse, because young mothers are often uneducated about effective parenting practices and are unable to secure employment.

Latina teenage pregnancies are also the result of a cultural prohibition on birth control. As previously mentioned, sexuality is rarely spoken of, and that includes the use of condoms and other forms of birth control. This may be due in part to the Catholic Church's prohibition on the use of birth control. Also, the male Latino may find condoms inhibit his sense of virility. Lastly, if the female uses birth control, she must admit to herself and others that she planned to engage in sexual relations, which makes her less pure than if sex just happens in the heat of the moment.

One other factor plays into the high percentage of Latina teenage births. Whereas other ethnic groups might choose to have an abortion or give up an unplanned pregnancy for adoption, these two options are not considered by Hispanics. The Catholic Church sees abortion as a mortal sin. And Hispanic families tend to welcome God's gift of a child with open arms.

Intervention Programs for Teenage Pregnancy

Many specialized programs have been created to deal with the issues of teen pregnancy. In locations where Spanish-speaking families are prevalent, these programs use bilingual and bicultural workers. The aim of these programs is to educate teens about caring for the unborn fetus, parenting the child after birth, and preventing future unplanned pregnancies. Some programs have financial incentives to encourage teens to prevent future pregnancies.

Another focus of these programs is to encourage teenaged girls to continue their education. Unfortunately, only 18% of young women under age 18 who bear children will complete high school. Pregnancy is cited as a major reason for female dropout rates (California Senate Office of Research, 1997). Without a high school diploma, these teens have few or no marketable skills, relegating them to minimum-wage jobs or welfare.

Long-term prevention of subsequent teen pregnancies seems to depend of several factors. One has to do with adequate information regarding sexuality, reproduction, and family planning methods. Chavez (1997) compared two programs that worked with pregnant teens. She measured program success on whether students became pregnant again within 12 months of completing the program. Of the two programs, the one that offered family planning and birth control education, peer-facilitated support groups and workshops, and field trips was more successful than the one that did not offer these services.

When dealing with Latinas, another factor should be emphasized: motivation to remain in school and plan for a career. If cultural tradition encourages young girls to get married and raise a family rather than attend college or live independently, teen pregnancy will continue to be acceptable.

In conclusion, if teenage pregnancy can be decreased, it is possible to at the same time decrease child abuse and neglect, which are often associated with teen pregnancy.

LATINO GANGS

Some people believe that gangs are part of Latino culture. This is far from the truth. As was mentioned previously, many Latinos join gangs as a way to reject the oppressed servant mentality that is often an accepted attitude among poor Latinos. Being part of a gang gives the adolescent a feeling of power and often leads to easy money, qualities that are in line with mainstream American culture. Greed and control are not typical of Hispanics, but they are characteristic of gang members.

Most gang members, in fact, were born in the U.S., and very few speak Spanish fluently. Gangs do not provide Mexican cultural awareness, pride, or cultural education, but gang association does provide relief from alienation and offers a type of strong family unit. Alienation from others and lack of social integration may be significant predictors of gang affiliation. The high rates of poverty among many Latinos may also be a factor influencing gang affiliation. Being in a gang may provide means of acquiring money, which allows the youth to buy material things and, at times, drugs. Latino families whose economic condition allows for the youth to have some personal spending money and material possessions comparable to mainstream youth tend to move out of dysfunctional neighborhoods that often produce gangs.

Dealing with Gangs

The most fruitful strategies for dealing with gangs are those that emphasize prevention and intervention rather than punishment. The fact that many students drop out of high school at age 14 may be a factor in gang affiliation, so perhaps this age should be raised to 18. Also, it might be useful if the role models of today, (i.e., rap stars, athletes, etc.) were to cease wearing gang attire and presenting gang mentality as "cool." Of course, until poverty is reduced, gangs will probably continue to exist. Likewise, this population must develop a value system in which education is a priority, because education is the path to economic success in the U.S. Chapter 6 addresses the importance of the educational system on the lives of Latinos.

The community itself must also participate in the reduction of gangs. Perhaps a neighborhood gang watch would help. Businesses could offer employment to gang members. Lastly, these youth might be helped by having their parents and society educate them on the beauty of Mexican culture so they might take pride in their heritage. Parents must be educated and supported in their efforts to control their children.

LATINOS AND SUBSTANCE ABUSE

Gang involvement is not the only deviant behavior observed in Latino youth. Substance abuse and other juvenile delinquency problems continue to increase among adolescents of all ethnicities, including Latinos. McQueen, et al., (2003) argue that Mexican-American adolescents may be more prone to substance abuse and other deviant behaviors because of the process of individuation that occurs during adolescence. Most would agree that by adolescence, teens typically become more autonomous and separate emotionally from their parents. However, Latino culture places a strong emphasis on interdependence. Given the central importance of the family among Mexican-Americans, the **individuation** process for a Latino teen might be experienced as maladaptive. In fact, McQueen, et al., (2003) demonstrated that an increase in separation from the family was related to an increase in substance abuse. As mentioned in Chapter 3, the acculturation process does tend to create difficulties for Latinos. For adolescents, the biggest issue is finding one's own identity as a person in mainstream culture without losing one's family and cultural identity. Substance abuse appears to serve as a behavior that in some way reduces the emotional distress related to this problem.

Even with adults, acculturation is related to alcohol abuse (Caetano, 1987). In addition, the family also influences whether Latinos abuse alcohol. It has been shown that parental and sibling drinking influences adolescent consumption of alcohol (Estrada et al., 1982; Guinn, 1978). In contrast, good family management by parents, communication between family members characterized by directness, reciprocity, and specificity, flexibility in handling stressors, and effective conflict resolution have been shown to reduce the risk for substance abuse.

Based on these factors, intervention programs for Latinos with substance and alcohol abuse problems might best focus on endeavors to strengthen ties to family, school, peers, and culture (Cervantes, 1993). Of course, alcohol- and drug-prevention programs must be tailored to the target population, so the role of acculturation must be dealt with when dealing with Latinos. Clearly, Latinos need to maintain cultural identity to maintain self-esteem and life-enhancing behaviors.

LATINOS AND DOMESTIC VIOLENCE

Intimate partner abuse is prevalent in the United States for all cultural groups, Latinos being no exception. There are some components of Latino culture that may contribute to the high prevalence of battering in this population. Many Latinas are isolated due to language barriers and cultural differences, and they often feel disconnected from medical care providers or feel threatened by police contact (especially if they are illegal immigrants). Others may be unaware of resources, unaware that spousal abuse is a crime, or believe that it would create a negative stigma on themselves if they told others about the abuse.

Because so many Latinos live in poverty, they may also be prone to live with spousal abuse because they lack economic self-sufficiency due to poor English skills, a poor employment history, and low educational attainment. As has been discussed previously, the focus in Latino culture to maintain a strong family unity may also influence domestic violence. An abused wife may feel unable to leave or set boundaries because of cultural mandates that prohibit a Latino woman from asserting power over her husband. Research suggests that about 85% of Latinas who were battered by their husbands grew up in homes where their fathers or stepfathers physically abused their mothers, and about 92% of Latino batterers observed the same in their childhood homes (Perilla,1999). Not only is spousal abuse among Latinos influenced by the cultural norm of familism, but it is influenced by the modeling of parents. The idea that Latina women should have respeto for their man also increases the likelihood of being abused and tolerating it.

This machismo among Latino men plays a part in abusive behaviors of all types, not just physical abuse. Machismo encourages Latino men to control, intimidate, and use male privilege in a marital relationship. Possessive love is also part of this machismo. This often takes the form of extreme jealousy—"a common rationalization batterers use as a reason for their violence" (Perilla, 1999, p. 120). These behaviors are all considered to be part of domestic violence.

Many of the Latino batterers claim they didn't know that their behavior was against the law and are surprised that there are consequences for it in the United States. Lack of consequences and being able to get away with spousal abuse are two reasons why it continues.

Interventions

In order to intervene effectively with Latino batterers and battered Latinas, human service workers must utilize Latino cultural elements. Because children are cherished in Latino homes, counselors must emphasize the damage that occurs to children when they witness violence. Both the mother and the father must be educated about the multigenerational aspect of domestic violence. Counselors can inquire about the parents' own childhoods and how they felt observing violence in their childhood homes.

Another strategy for helping Latinos involved in domestic violence is to educate them about the historical and social conditions of their country of origin and how that might be influencing their current behaviors in the United States. They might be encouraged to reinvent their culture in the U.S., blending both old and new traditions. The Latino male can be made aware of the false roles and expectations that have been imposed on men and women in his culture, and can learn to emphasize the positive aspects of the machista ethos. The Latino male must also be educated to recognize and accept the fundamental human rights of his partner and children to a life free of terror, violence, and abuse. The Latina woman can learn about resources, laws, and options available in this country. She must also learn that she has the right to have her decisions respected by others (Perilla, 1999, p. 129).

LATINOS AND AIDS

According to the Centers for Disease Control (2000), the national incidence rate of AIDS among Latinos is more than three times that of non-Latino Whites

(23% vs. 7%, respectively). Latina women are five times as likely as non-Latino White women to die from AIDS, and Latino men are twice as likely as non-Latino White men to die from the disease (National Alliance for Hispanic Health, 2000). It has been estimated that about 40% of Latino AIDS cases are among men of Mexican origin, and 86% of these men are born in Mexico (California Health and Human Services Agency, 2002). The rate of AIDS is especially high in labor camps among Latino men.

Why is the prevalence of AIDS so high in the Latino community? Some have suggested that Latinos are less informed about the AIDS virus and its modes of transmission (Hardy, 1990, McCaig, & Hardy and Winn, 1991). Urizar & Winkleby (2003) found that lack of education about AIDS is highest among Latinos with low educational attainment, elderly Latinos, and Latinos who didn't have regular contact with a doctor. Many believed that AIDS could be spread like other communicable disorders such as the cold and the flu.

Interventions

Obviously, intervention strategies must include education about how AIDS in transmitted, how to engage in safer sexual practices (use of condoms, one sexual partner, avoidance of intercourse), and how to get tested. Latinos must be educated about how the virus can be transmitted to their partners and how it creates problems in the family. They must know that not only gay men get AIDS; it is observed in all populations. Latinos must understand how they may be contributing to the decline of the Latino population by not practicing safe sex.

GLOSSARY OF TERMS

Ataque de Nervios: an attack of the nerves, with symptoms often confused with panic disorder, generalized anxiety disorder, or major depressive disorder.

Individuation: The process of becoming independent and autonomous that usually begins in adolescence. It is a form of emotional separation from one's parents.

REFERENCES

American Psychiatric Association. (1994). *Diagnostic and Statistical Manual of Mental Disorders* (4th ed.). Washington, D.C.: Author.

Becerra H., & Alvarez, F. (2001). Latinos make big census gains. *Los Angeles Times.* May 10, 2001.

Caetano, R. (1987). Acculturation and drinking patterns among U.S. Hispanics. *British Journal of the Addictions, 82,* 789-799.

California Health and Human Services Agency. (2002). *California and the HIV/AIDS epidemic: The state of the state report.* Sacramento: Office of AIDS.

California Senate Office of Research. (1997). *California strategies to address teenage pregnancy.* Sacramento, CA: Senate Publications.

Centers for Disease Control. (2000). *HIV/AIDS among Hispanics in the United States.* Retrieved November 12, 2002, from http://www.cdc.gov/hiv/pubs/facts/hispanics/htm.

Cervantes, R. (1993). The Hispanic family intervention program: An empirical approach to substance abuse prevention. In R. Sanchez-Mayers, B. Kail, & T. Watts (Eds.), *Hispanic Substance Abuse.* Springfield, ILL: Charles C. Thomas.

Chavez, J. (1997). *Subsequent pregnancies within teen pregnancy programs.* An Independent Study Project submitted to Kristi Kanel as partial fulfillment of the Bachelor of Science Degree in Human Services. California State University, Fullerton.

Delgado, M. (1998). *Social service in Latino communities: Research and strategies.* New York: Haworth.

Estrada, A., Rabow, J., & Watts, R. (1982). Alcohol use among Hispanic adolescents: A preliminary report. *Hispanic Journal of Behavioral Sciences, 4,* 3, 339-351.

Falicov, C. J. (1982). Mexican families. In M. McGoldrick, J. K. Pearce, & J. Giordano (Eds.). *Ethnicity and Family therapy.* New York: Guilford.

Guinn, C. (1978). Alcohol use among Mexican American youth. *Journal of School Health, 48,* 90-91.

Hardy, A. M. (1990). National health interview survey data on adult knowledge of AIDS in the United States. *Public Health Reports, 105,* 629-634.

Kanel, K. (2002). Mental Health Needs of Spanish-Speaking Latinos in Southern California. *Hispanic Journal of Behavioral Sciences, 24* (1), 74-91.

Koss-Chioino, J. D. (1999). Depression Among Puerto Rican Women: Culture, Etiology and Diagnosis. *Hispanic Journal of Behavioral Sciences, 21* (3), 330-350.

Liebowitz, M. R., Salman, E., Jusion, C. M., Garfinkel, R., Street, L., Cardenas, D. L., Silvestre, J., Fyer, A. J., Carrasco, J. L., Davies, S., Guarnaccia, P., & Klein, D. (1994). Ataque de Nervios and Panic Disorder. *American Journal of Psychiatry, 151*(6), 871-875.

Lopez, S. R., Grover, K. P., Holland, D., Johnson, M. J., Kain, C. D., Kanel, K., et al. (1989). Development of culturally sensitive psychotherapists. *Professional Psychology: Research and Practice, 20,* 369-376.

McCaig, L. F., Hardy, A. M., & Winn, D. M. (1991). Knowledge about AIDS and

HIV in the U.S. adult population: Influence of the local incidence of AIDS. *American Journal of Public Health, 81*, 1591-1595.

McDonnell, P. J., (2001). Mexicans change face of U.S. demographics. *Los Angeles Times,* May 5, 2001.

McQueen, A., Getz, J. G., & Bray, J. H. (2003). Acculturation, Substance Use, and Deviant Behavior: Examining Separation and Family Conflict as Mediators. *Child Development, 74*, 6, 1737-1750.

National Alliance for Hispanic Health. (2000). *Quality health services for Hispanics: The cultural competency component.* Rockville, MD: U.S. Department of Health and Human Services, Office of Minority Health, Substance Abuse and Mental Health Services Administration.

Oquendo, M. A. (1995). Differential Diagnosis of Ataque De Nervios. *American Journal of Orthopsychiatry, 65* (1), 60-64.

Orangewood Children's Foundation & Center for Collaboration for Children at California State University, Fullerton. (2000). *The sixth annual report on the conditions of children in Orange County.* Sponsored by the Orange County 2000 Board of Supervisors. Orange County, CA: Author.

Perilla, J. L. (1999). Domestic Violence as a Human Rights Issue: The Case of Immigrant Latinos. *Hispanic Journal of Behavioral Sciences, 21*, 2, 107-133.

Remez, L. (1991). Rates of Adolescent Pregnancy and Childbearing are High among Mexico-Born Mexican Americans. *Family Planning Perspectives, 23*, 2, 88-90.

Rubio, M., Urdaneta, M., & Doyle, J. L. Psychopathological Reaction Patterns in the Antilles Command. *US Armed Forces Medical Journal 6*, 1767-1772.

Salazar, R. A., & Valdez, J. N. (2000). The need for specialized clinical training mental health service delivery to Latinos. *Academic Exchange Quarterly, 4*(4), 92-98.

Salman, E., Liebowitz, M. R., Guarnaccia, P. J., Jusino, C. M., Garfinkel, R., Street, L., Cardenas, D. L., Silvestre, J., Fyer, A. J., Carrasco, J. L., Davies, S. O., & Klein, D. F. (1998). Subtypes of Ataques de Nervios: The Influence of Coexisting Psychiatric Diagnosis. *Culture, Medicine and Psychiatry, 22*, 231-244.

Schechter, D. S., Marshall, R., Salman, E., Goetz, D., Davies, S., & Liebowitz, M. R. (2000). Ataque de Nervios and History of Childhood Trauma. *Journal of Traumatic Stress, 13* (3), 529-534.

Urizar, G. G., & Winkleby, M. A. (2003). AIDS Knowledge Among Latinos: Finding from a Community and Agricultural Labor Camp Survey. *Hispanic Journal of Behavioral Sciences, 25*, 3, 295-311.

U.S. Census Bureau. (2001). *Race, Hispanic or Latino.* Available from www.census.gov.

CHAPTER 5

Social Welfare Delivery to Latinos

INTRODUCTION

The social welfare system includes a variety of services for children, parents, and the elderly. As with other ethnic groups, Hispanics utilize these services to assist them with a multitude of needs. When providing these services to Latinos, especially those who only speak Spanish, social workers and advocates should maintain a culturally sensitive stance. At times, this is hard to do, because as has been noted earlier, the values of Latinos often conflict with the values of governmental institutions. The **social welfare agencies** of particular concern for human service workers provide child protective services, financial services, medical services, and services for the elderly. The types of people often in need of social welfare programs consist of abused children, abusive parents, those living in poverty, and those elderly persons who are living in abusive conditions or who suffer from major medical illnesses, such as Alzheimer's disease.

Latinos who only speak Spanish often fear social welfare agencies due to **illegal immigrant status**. They worry that their illegal status will be reported to government officials by social workers and, therefore, are reluctant to seek the help they need. Ignorance of how the social welfare system operates, as well as difficulties in communication due to language barriers, may also hinder necessary utilization of social services, despite a great need for these services. High rates of poverty among Latinos in the U.S. indicate that there is a large need among this population for financial aid, housing aid, medical aid, and child care assistance. Additionally, many Latinos immigrating from other countries engage in parenting practices that are deemed abusive by U.S. standards and, therefore, create a need for intervention by the social welfare system.

CHILDREN'S SERVICES

Most cities have a separate division in their social welfare system that deals specifically with the protection and welfare of children. Because of the passage of the Child Abuse Prevention and Treatment Act in 1974, all states in the U.S. are required to adopt specific procedures to identify, treat, and prevent child abuse (Crosson-Tower, 1999, p. 13). At times, the typical manner in which Latinos (especially new immigrants) discipline their children is considered abusive. Physical punishment is used as the primary method of regulating children in most Latino families. This contrasts with American social workers' expectations that parents use communication, restriction, and compromise as the major forms of parental discipline. Another problem facing Spanish-speaking families is the fact that, many times, small children are raised by older children because both parents must work long hours to support the family. This can lead to lack of attention and nurturance, as well as to physical abuse from older siblings who don't have the skills necessary to properly parent younger siblings.

When a situation is reported to **Child Protective Services**, Latino parents are often confused. They don't understand why outsiders are interfering with their home life, which is usually private in Latin American countries. They often don't perceive their discipline as abusive, and were often disciplined in the same manner by their own parents when they were children.

EXAMPLE: A 35-year-old woman from Nicaragua was reported to Child Protective Services because she had tied up her 11-year-old daughter with duct tape. The daughter had evidence of adhesive tape on her wrists, mouth, and neck. Additionally, the mother had hit the daughter over her entire body with a wooden spoon for misbehavior. The mother stated that in her country it was typical to beat children with wooden spoons and put tape on their mouths to keep them quiet. However, because this beating of her daughter left many bruises, Child Protective Services removed the daughter from the home. The mother was shocked, angered, and unable to see that she had done anything wrong. She needed to be educated about the laws in the U.S., which regard any discipline that leaves bruises to be child abuse and, therefore, maltreatment. The social worker emphasized the reality of the laws rather than moralized about the evil nature of the disciplinary practice. Later, when the mother and daughter attended counseling, the therapist encouraged both mother and daughter to communicate their feelings about what had happened. The mother was later able to share that as a child she didn't like being beaten with a spoon and that it made her angry with her mother. She could understand that her own daughter also didn't like this type of discipline. Since she didn't want her own daughter to be angry at her, the mother accepted that other disciplinary practices might be more beneficial in creating the type of mother-daughter relationship she never had, but desired, with her own mother.

Another example demonstrates how putting a teenager in charge of smaller children can lead to child abuse.

Example: A 16-year-old daughter was given the responsibility to take care of her 6-year-old sister after school until the mother returned from work at 4:00 p.m. The father also worked until about that time. One day, the 16-year-old hit her sister and left bruises. The father was actually the stepfather of the 16-year-old and the natural father of the 6-year-old. A teacher at the 6-year-old girl's school reported the bruises as child abuse to Child Protective Services. The parents were required to find alternative babysitting for the 6-year-old. Although the parents didn't actually abuse the daughter, they were held liable for the abuse that happened to her.

Treatment of Physical Abuse

In working with Spanish-speaking families, there may need to be some alteration in the way interventions are practiced. First, as always, it is best to conduct sessions in Spanish whenever possible. This ensures that the parents understand the material presented. Much of the treatment for abusive parents is parent education. This includes presentations, usually in a group, of normal child development and appropriate expectations, as well as effective parenting practices, such as implementation of positive reinforcement and response cost method.

Because these types of parenting methods are not common in traditional Latino homes, where blind obedience is expected due to respeto for the parents, there may be resistance by the parents to practice them. The parenting educator, counselors, and social workers must emphasize that the parents need to make adjustments to their parenting style to meet the demands of American culture. By framing the new parenting practices as a necessary cultural adjustment, the parents are saved from some shame and humiliation; it's not that they are being told they are bad parents, just that things have to be different because they are in a different country and the laws are different.

Treatment may also consist of having the perpetrator share a bit about his or her own childhood and the effects that abusive behavior had on his or her own self-esteem. If the client wasn't abused, then the counselors and social workers must explore why the parent becomes so angry with the child. Issues of power and control must be examined. Perhaps the parent feels that because the child speaks English, the power differential is unequal, and the abusive behavior is unconsciously designed to ensure that the parent maintains the power base.

At other times, marital problems may need to be dealt with, but only indirectly. The counselor or social worker can point out how important it is for the couple to pull their resources together for the sake of the children and the family. This is a delicate matter that must be dealt with nonjudgementally. Remember, the children keep the family together. Latino parents are devastated when a child is taken from the home. Keep the focus on practical steps necessary to reunite the family. Case plans must be specific and attainable financially and logistically. For example, if a parent works at a factory during the hours of 3-11 p.m., it would be inappropriate to insist that he attend a parenting group on Thursday night from 6-9 p.m. Alternatives must be considered.

Referrals to groups with other Hispanic parents accused of physical abuse are very helpful. These groups can deal with cultural variations in parenting practices and often help the parents feel less vilified.

NEGLECT

Physical abuse is not the only type of child abuse observed in the Hispanic population. In fact, **general neglect** is more prevalent than any other type of child abuse. It includes the lack of provision of adequate nutrition, clothing, shelter, medical care, and supervision. It is often associated with poverty and lack of medical insurance, drug and alcohol abuse, ignorance, cultural diversity, and depression and apathy in the parents. When Latinos are not in the U.S. legally, they may be hesitant to access needed services that ensure that their children are appropriately provided for; hence these parents are often guilty of child neglect. This is reportable under child abuse laws.

Intervention with Neglect Cases

If neglect is simply due to poverty, social workers often need only connect the family to welfare services, such as financial aid, food stamps, medical care, and housing assistance. Other cases of neglect require education about proper nutrition and clothing. When the neglect is due to drug abuse by a parent, drug abuse treatment is required. Sometimes, a neglectful parent is very depressed and apathetic. This person may need individual counseling or medication to reduce depression levels.

Example: A 27-year-old Mexican-American single mother was improperly feeding her children. The children complained to their teacher that they were always hungry. When asked if their mother fed them, they said yes, but the food gave them stomachaches and diarrhea. The social worker discovered that the mother served the children grease in all their meals, (she didn't drain the grease from hamburger meat before adding sauce). Treatment included sending a public health nurse to the home to teach the mother how to cook and make meals more appetizing to the children.

SEXUAL ABUSE

Sexual abuse of children is an unfortunate reality in our society. This type of abuse exists among all ethnic groups. When a social worker or counselor interfaces with a Hispanic family in which sexual abuse has become an issue, certain factors must be taken into consideration. Of course, many of these factors are not unique to Latinos.

The Latino Marital Relationship

As stated earlier, the relationship between husband and wife in Latino homes is often child based. Intimacy, both sexual and emotional, is not emphasized. This often leads to marital dissatisfaction. Remember the **double standard** regarding sexuality in this culture. If a woman enjoys sex too much, she may be looked upon as a puta (whore). If she doesn't respond sexually, her husband may feel sexually frustrated and deprived. Since matters of sex are seldom spoken of in this culture, the wife and husband have no way of addressing issues of deprivation and sexual needs. This may precipitate the husband to seek sexual gratification elsewhere, either with another woman, or with a daughter.

Machista and the Sexual Perpetrator

Oftentimes, the father or stepfather (the two most likely child sexual-abuse **perpetrators)**, are relegated to low-paying, manual jobs, which may create low self-esteem and feelings of powerlessness. Without a chance for advancement, these men, who have been taught that males must be virile and in control (**machista),** may seek ways of feeling powerful and in control. The sexual abuse of a child may satisfy that need.

Objectification of Women

Throughout history, men have objectified women. That is, men have not con-sidered women to be equal humans, worthy of the same respect, dialogue, and treatment as men. This objectification of women is particularly strong in the Latin tradition. It hasn't always been a negative phenomenon. Women were often put on a pedestal and treated as the sacred and puritanical virgin to be cherished and protected. However, this same type of unrealistic perspective toward women has also led to the prevalence of sexual assaults against women. In the case of sexual assault against children, this **objectification** is more pronounced, especially in Hispanic homes, where children are not considered to have a voice. A Hispanic man often thinks of his wife and children as his property to do with what he feels. The idea that a child has an identity and the right to personal space is not typically part of the mindset of Latino parents. The wife may even believe that her children should endure sexual relations with their father. Perhaps she, herself, was abused as a child and perceives it to be within normal limits of acceptable practice.

Intervention in Cases of Sexual Abuse

The intervention in sexual abuse cases for Latino families is not very different from that with other cultures. Those involved in sexual abuse usually use defense mechanisms such as denial, rationalization, minimization, and repression to cover up their intense shame and humiliation. This means that the social worker and counselor will have a difficult time assisting family members to accept that the behavior was indeed abusive and that is really existed.

Children who are sexually abused need to be told it is not acceptable and that it wasn't their fault in any way, regardless of what the parents told them about culpability. In Hispanic families, the focus on respeto may be stronger than in mainstream culture. Therefore, the sexually abused child may feel intense fear in disclosing abuse, as it would be considered disrespectful to "tell on his or her parents." Also, in order to control the child, the perpetrator often tells the child that he or she must not tell because it would be disrespectful. This belief in respeto is extremely difficult for counselors to alter. It may take years of therapy, group therapy, and conversations with clergy to help the girl or woman abused as a child realize that it is acceptable to feel anger and be unhappy with her father, stepfather, brother, or grandfather for having sexually abused her.

EXAMPLE: A 59-year-old Latina has been in therapy for more than 15 years trying to deal with her childhood sexual abuse. Her father forced oral sex and intercourse on her. Also, her brother was physically abusive. This client feels extreme fear and shame for disclosing the abuse and for blaming the perpetrators. She feels that she is being disrespectful and that they will punish her, even though they are now dead. Her childhood belief that she must be respectful remained with her for more than 50 years.

Play therapy may also help a child who was sexually abused. Family therapy in which the parents directly speak with the child may not be wise, as this conflicts with the deep cultural tradition of the parent having supreme authority over the child. Also, the child may feel disrespectful for causing the parents shame. Instead, therapists should work individually with the child and send the parents to groups with other perpetrating parents.

These groups should be supportive and confrontational. It may not be effective to have both the husband and wife together, as this may conflict with the cultural tradition of the husband being the family leader. Privacy may be important to preserve family structure. In fact, focus should be on family structure. The parents need to be shown that having sex with a child creates a faulty family structure; that behavior puts the child on the same level as the parents, which inhibits the kind of respeto needed for families to function properly.

Marital therapy should concentrate on how to preserve the family, if possible. Sometimes, however, depending on the financial situation, level of acculturation, and desire of the **non-perpetrating parent**, separation may be a possibility. Many Hispanic couples choose this over divorce. Both should be encouraged to express their feelings to each other openly. However, keep in mind, this is not easy, as this type of communication is unusual in Latino marriages. It is better to discuss practical issues when the couple is together, and save sexual abuse issues for when the perpetrator is alone.

SERVICES FOR THE ELDERLY

There are many programs and services for the elderly population, because they have special needs due to aging, such as poor health and financial issues. Hispanic elderly tend to underutilize social welfare services in general. This may be due in large part to cultural insensitivity by social welfare workers. Culturally competent practice with elderly Latinos will become increasingly vital in the coming decade. It is estimated that there will be an unprecedented growth in the elderly Latino population in the next ten years. The National Council of La Raza (NCLR, 1991) reports that this population is growing at a faster rate than the non-Latino population and is estimated to reach 6.3 percent of the total elderly population by the year 2010. However, unlike the general population, elderly Latinos only account for 5.2 percent of the total Latino population. Nearly 6 out of 10 elderly Latinos are native-born, with Mexican-Americans comprising 48 percent of all Latinos in the U.S.; Cuban Americans, 18 percent; Puerto Ricans, 11 percent; and other Latinos, 34 percent. It has been predicted by the U.S. Bureau of the Census (1992) that there will be a 200% increase in elderly Hispanics in the U.S. Unfortunately, these elderly Latinos are among the least-educated elderly group in the U.S., with slightly over one-third with less than five years schooling, and about 40% unable to speak English.

These figures certainly suggest the need for human service workers to be aware of the special needs of the elderly Latino when providing services. In particular, social welfare workers must consider 1) the socio-economic status of elderly Latinos, 2) the bio-psychosocial aspects of aging and issues of cultural relevance in gerontological theories to the Latino elderly, 3) the fundamental principles of culturally competent social work practice with elderly Latinos, and 4) the ecological perspective to exemplify the relevance of culture and ethnicity in culturally competent practice with elderly Latinos (Applewhite, 1998).

Economic Issues Facing Elderly Latinos

The poverty rates for elderly Latinos is estimated at 20.6%, twice that of elderly Whites in this country. This may be due to early retirement because of poor health, as well as to low-paying jobs because of minimal education. Elderly Latinos are less likely than other elderly Americans to receive Social Security or private pensions and, therefore, depend more on **Supplementary Security Income** *(*SSI) and public assistance programs. Unfortunately, they are often ineligible to receive even SSI due to immigration status.

Elderly Latinos have greater unmet medical needs due to the inability to afford proper care. Some erroneously believe they will be cared for by extended family and are less likely to turn to formal services and programs (Applewhite, 1998). Hispanic older persons show a higher prevalence of diabetes than non-Hispanic Whites. This particular disease disadvantages this group because it is often related to other disabilities, such as lower extremity amputations, vascular disease, blindness, and stroke. It is also linked with greater dependency, such as the need for assistance in performing basic and instrumental activities of daily living (Villa, 1999).

In dealing with the elderly Latino population, social workers must be aware of the various reasons for the high rates of poverty in elderly Hispanics. The lack of savings and preparation for retirement are due largely to language and cultural barriers, as well as to a distrust of banks, lack of pension plans, and absence of extra cash, which is often sent to family abroad (Freedman, 1997). This population must be encouraged to plan for their own retirement and medical needs. Programs must be created and strengthened to educate this group on proper medical care, including disease prevention. It is certain that community-based health and long-term care programs that offer basic health and assistance with daily living activities must be developed. This may help avoid the need and expense of institutionalization (Villa, 1999). Additionally, Social Security benefits for undocumented workers may have to be instituted. These workers usually pay into the Social Security system and should collect on their investment as the general population does.

Because elderly Latinos are often distrustful of American doctors and the health care system in general, they sometimes seek out the services of curanderos at botanicas. As the research study demonstrated in Chapter 3, this is not a common practice in Southern California, but Delagado (1998) describes it as common in New York by the elderly Puerto Rican population. It is possible that certain botanica owners might take advantage of the elderly, in a sense preying on their ignorance and taking their money for services that don't help rid the individual of serious health problems. These botanicas aren't the only institution that may financially abuse the elderly Hispanic person. The medical profession and assisted-living institutions often abuse the elderly population in general. Due to language difficulties, Spanish-speaking elderly Latinos do not receive comparable services to those who speak fluent English, simply because doctors and other service providers cannot communicate adequately with them. The fact that elderly Latinos often don't understand the system and cannot communicate their needs increases the likelihood of abuse by providers.

Gerontology Theories as Related to Hispanics

It is possible that current theories about aging fail to consider the cultural variations between Hispanics and the general population. There are widespread differences in aging patterns between elderly Latinos and the general aging population, such as poorer health in Latinos and lower life expectancy (Applewhite, 1998). The culturally competent practitioner must examine various cultural responses to aging in order to better understand why these differences exist.

Elderly Latinos usually do better when they live in a nurturing environment that may include family and community. This natural support system increases the elderly Latino's sense of competence and relatedness. This connection with the community helps them experience pride and dignity, which could affect mental and physical health. Interventions that incorporate natural support systems in the community are essential when dealing with the elderly Latino. The key focus for culturally competent practice is to build trust and rapport, and reduce fearfulness, suspiciousness, and pessimism, about social services.

FINANCIAL ASSISTANCE

Financial assistance includes cash, medical care, housing, and food. The populations typically eligible for federal, state, or county aid include children, the elderly, and the disabled. Hispanics who meet these requirements often face certain problems that other ethnic groups do not. The biggest impediment to Latinos receiving financial assistance is their immigration status. In particular, Mexicans who migrate to the U.S. often lack the legal papers that other immigrants, such as Asians, Cubans, and Middle Easterners, have.

As has been stated earlier, many Hispanics live under the poverty level. Surprisingly, many of those families do not apply for needed financial aid or any type of government assistance. They are often afraid of being deported, even though their children, born here, would be eligible for assistance. Even authorized Mexican immigrants often bypass needed assistance because of ignorance of the system and strong work ethic values. When they do apply for welfare, they may have communication problems due to language barriers. Also, they often face discrimination by human service workers who may believe that unauthorized Mexican immigrants use welfare inappropriately. Many people hold negative views about Latino values that encourage large families, even in the face of poverty. Indeed, the Illegal Immigration Reform and Immigrant Responsibility Act passed in 1996 by President Clinton greatly affected this population, as it almost eliminated food stamps and MediCal to illegal and legal immigrants (Marcelli & Heer, 1998).

Why do Mexicans Often Live in Poverty?

This question has frustrated social workers for many years. In part, this may be due to a value system that puts work ahead of education. As mentioned earlier, the Latino culture values large families, which creates more family expenses. Also, parents of these families often grew up in extreme poverty and might perceive their standard of living in the U.S. as good by comparison. They need to understand that this country doesn't allow children to be deprived of food, medical care, and appropriate shelter and clothing. Prejudice by human service workers might inhibit the education this population needs about accessing services for their children. It isn't fair to deprive children of proper care just because their parents make decisions based on different cultural values.

While many think illegal immigrants come to this country to use the welfare system, in fact, this is not true. Despite the fact that 40% of **unauthorized Mexican Immigrants** (UMIS) live in poverty, they are 11% less likely than other ethno-racial groups, and 14% less likely than U.S.-born citizens to use welfare. U.S. citizens of Latino origin use welfare benefits 55% more often than UMIS, and White immigrants use welfare benefits 30% more than UMIS. Remember, if a UMIS has a child born in the U.S., that family is entitled to food stamps, MediCal, and Temporary Assistance for Needy Families (TANF) (Marcelli & Heer, 1998). These statistics indicate underutilization of welfare services by UMIS.

What Can be Done?

The next chapter deals with educational issues and their relation to poverty. In addition to encouraging Latinos to attain higher education, which would help them secure better-paying jobs, human service workers should better educate this population about their rights to financial assistance. This might best be done by focusing on the needs of children and how they deserve proper food and medical care. Human service workers must present themselves as friendly and personable, and it certainly helps if they can speak a little Spanish. Speaking the same language as the client increases trust. Remember, Spanish-speaking clients tend to be wary of government programs and may fear that their illegal status will be discovered.

It is a good idea to let Latino clients know that if they don't provide proper care for their children—even if it means receiving financial assistance—their children could be taken from them under child neglect laws. This may serve as motivation for them to seek assistance.

It is also necessary to advise Latinos to save money for retirement. They should be encouraged to think about their future to prevent poverty in old age. A little education about banks might help them trust the system. The issue of a poor elderly Latino population will continue to be a big problem if retirement is not addressed in the working years.

GLOSSARY OF TERMS

Child Protective Services: a part of the social welfare system that serves to prevent and manage situations in which child abuse and neglect are reported to officials.

Double Standard: the tendency to regard acceptable behaviors as different for men and women.

General Neglect: occurs when a child fails to receive basic needs such as shelter, food, clothing, and medical care.

Illegal Immigrant Status: a person who has come to the U.S. without authorized documents, passports, or visas.

Machista: a term that refers to the Latino male's desire to be seen as powerful and virile.

Non-perpetrating parents: the parent who did not directly abuse their children but lives with the parent who did.

Objectification: the attitude and behaviors that lead women to be treated like property to be sexually used for a man's pleasure.

Perpetrators: parents who have abused their children.

Supplementary Security Income: a federal- and state-funded financial assistance program designed for the disabled and poor elderly.

Unauthorized Mexican Immigrants (UMIS): a term that has recently been used to describe Mexicans who come to the U.S. without legal documents.

Social Welfare agencies: organizations that serve clients who have a variety needs. Some of the populations that receive social welfare assistance include children, the elderly, the disabled, and the poor.

REFERENCES

Applewhite, S. L. (1998). Culturally competent practice with elderly Latinos. *Journal of Gerontological Social Work, 30*, ?, 1-13.

Crosson-Tower, C. (1999). *Understanding Child Abuse and Neglect* (4th Ed.). Boston, MA: Allyn and Bacon.

Freedman, D. (1997). *Hispanics face issues of social security and retirement savings.* Hearst Newspapers. Nov. 2, 1997. Retrieved electronically1/20/99 from http://www.latinolink.com/news/news97/1102nhis.htm.

Marcelli, E. A., & Heer, D. M. (1998). The unauthorized Mexican immigrant population and welfare in Los Angeles County: a comparative statistical analysis. *Sociological Perspectives, 41*, 2, 279-303.

Orangewood Children's Foundation & Center for Collaboration for Children at California State University, Fullerton. (2000). *The sixth annual report on the conditions of children in Orange County.* Sponsored by the Orange County 2000 Board of Supervisors. Orange County, CA: Author.

Villa, V. (1999). The demography, health and economic status of minority elderly populations: Implications for aging programs and services. *GCM Journal, Spring 1999*, 5-8.

CHAPTER 6

The Educational System and Latinos

INTRODUCTION

Low educational achievement has been linked with many social problems, such as poverty, drug abuse, domestic violence, child abuse, and crime. One hypothesis is that a good education can prevent many other social problems, such as teen pregnancy, crime, drug and alcohol abuse, domestic violence, and poverty. In other words, many of the issues presented in the previous chapters could be prevented if the parents and children were to attain higher education.

While some Latinos in the U.S. are highly educated, as discussed in Chapter 2, many are undereducated by American standards. Interestingly, the elementary school system in Mexico is very stringent and demanding compared to U.S. schools. However, many Mexicans are encouraged to leave school by grade three to help the family financially. Those who do stay in school often do not finish high school or attend college. Likewise, many Latinos in the U.S. do not finish high school or complete a college education. This leaves this population relegated to lower-income, non-professional jobs. Human service workers in all professions must be aware of a variety of factors related to Latino education in order to best provide services.

VALUES ABOUT EDUCATION AND WORK

Not all people of Latino descent hold the same values about education. This may be more of a class issue than an ethnic issue. In other words, Latinos raised in a lower **socioeconomic status** may be less inclined to emphasize the importance of education than those raised in middle- to upper-class homes. This is probably true of all ethnicities. As has been discussed earlier, most of the Latinos in the U.S. are of Mexican descent. Most of the Mexican immigrants come from lower socioeconomic status. Hence, we turn to this group when discussing education and work ethics.

While most Latinos would certainly verbalize that education is important, in fact, many Latino children are either discouraged from completing high school and college, or they receive very little support from parents to do so. These parents are often very busy working and raising several other children and simply do not have time to be involved in schooling. Also, the parents often do not speak English and feel incompetent to be involved. Lastly, because Mexican families are often living in poverty, parents insist that the children work at a young age in order to contribute financially to the family. Even when children move out on their own, they often are obligated to help out their family financially. This puts an extra burden on adult children who may wish to attend college.

Many Spanish-speaking families believe there is nothing wrong with working a low-paying job as long as it is honest work. Dignity is found in a hard day's work for fair pay. The saying *"pobre pero honesto"* (poor but honest) fits here. As long as the community is aware that the family works hard and provides the basics for the children, the family is perceived as valuable. If a child leaves home to go off to college and doesn't help support the family, the child may be seen as disrespectful and the parents may be shamed. A child who is in college is not valued as highly as a child who works hard to help support the family.

A Comparison of American and Latino Educational Values

Once a Latino child from a Spanish-speaking family enters elementary school, he or she faces certain obstacles. One, of course, is language. Recently, bilingual education in school was terminated. This means that lessons are no longer taught in Spanish. However, if the teacher can speak Spanish or has a teacher's aid that can, children sometimes get materials translated for them. There are other factors that can inhibit a Spanish-speaking child from attaining high educational performance. Certain American traits and values differ from those of Latinos. Following is an adaptation of a chart presented by Kanel (2000b), a professor of English in Japan. He suggests that differences between Japanese learners and American learners can be due in part to cultural differences on various dimensions. He also points out that these traits are generalizations and may be debatable and/or in a state of change. The author has utilized some of these traits to suggest differences between Latinos and Americans. Educators may wish to keep some of these differences in mind in order to maintain a more-realistic expectation of Latinos in school situations.

Table 6.1 Comparison of Latino and American Values

LATINOS	AMERICANS
Harmony of the group	Freedom of the individual
Consensus	Independence
Conformity	Self-centeredness
Ascribed respect	Earned respect
Hierarchy	Equality
Obedience	Assertiveness
Coercion	Rights
Intuition	Logic
Shame	Guilt
Modesty	Pride
Self-sacrifice	Self-indulgence
Reticence	Proactive
Effort	Results
Process	Performance
Suppression of originality/creativity	Critical thinking
Emotional	Intellectual
Inward	Outgoing
Humility	Confidence
Passiveness	Activeness
Authoritarianism	Democracy

Adapted from Kanel, K.R. (2000) with permission.

The reader will note the many differences between the two cultures and how these traits may affect the Latino learner in an American school system. Not only does a child from a Spanish-speaking family need to learn English, but he or she also must adapt to American culture. This often creates confusion and dissent within the family. It is no wonder that Latino parents often do not want to have anything to do with the schools their children attend.

PARENTAL INVOLVEMENT AND EDUCATIONAL ACHIEVEMENT

It has been proposed by many researchers that parental involvement in a child's education is paramount to academic achievement (Connell, Spencer, & Aber, 1994). They hypothesize that perceived parental involvement leads to several outcomes and present a model for understanding academic achievement (see diagram 6.1 below). Perceived parental involvement refers to students' experience of their families dedicating psychological resources to them (p. 495).

Diagram 6.1

Perceived Parental Involvement >
    Perceived Competence/Efficacy >
        Emotional and Behavioral Engagement >
            Either Negative or Positive Outcome, depending on whether parental involvement was perceived by the student.

This model has been adapted by the author.

Negative outcomes include low attendance, low test scores, low grades, suspension, and retention. Positive outcomes include high attendance, high test scores, and high grades.

Parental involvement in a child's schooling may also produce academic success, because teachers may provide increased attention to students whose parents make themselves known on campus. Anecdotal stories confirm that when parents are active members in the PTA (parent-teacher association), students do better in school. This may also be because these same parents take time to be involved with their child's homework and other school activities.

Home Environment and IQ

Studies have supported the idea that IQ in young children is related to various home environment factors. IQ scores usually measure **cognitive competence**, which frequently results in increased academic performance. In a study of 3-year-olds (Bradley & Caldwell, 1980), it was found that the responsivity of the mother correlated significantly with IQ scores. This suggests that young children develop intellectual capacity when mothers are present in the home and respond to children regularly. This was especially true for female children. Responsivity includes behaviors such as involvement in play with the child, talking with the child, and engaging in behaviors that meet the child's needs as requested by the child. It is quite possible that in Latino homes in which a mother must care for many children, **maternal responsivity** is low. Often, older siblings are put in charge of younger children, and these older children can't adequately provide the kind of responsivity that a mother could provide. This could lead to lowered cognitive competence. Also, remember that because many Latinos live in poverty, many mothers must work outside the home, which necessarily reduces their ability to be present to provide maternal responsivity. Lastly, the focus in traditional Latino families is to provide basic necessities, such as food and a clean home for children. Engaging in dialogue, reading, and playing with a child is not traditionally considered good parenting according to this culture. Unfortunately, this lack of maternal responsivity may lead to lowered cognitive competence, hence lowered school performance. Human service workers can share this information with their Latino clients and encourage more maternal involvement with young children by mothers.

Other factors have been found to be significantly correlated to higher IQ scores, including organization of the environment, play materials, and variety of stimulation. Due to poverty, many of these factors are deficient in many Latino homes. Also, time is a factor in providing a child with stimulation, something that a home with four or more children often lacks. To the extent that these factors can be provided to children, their cognitive competence will increase, thereby increasing their likelihood of academic success. Teachers, social workers, and counselors can all work together to encourage Latino parents to incorporate some of these behaviors with their children. This may have the ultimate effect of reducing high school drop out rates and increasing college success among Latinos.

Indeed, it has been supported by studies that parental attitudes about education determine the academic success of their children (Ebener, Lara-Alecio, & Irby, 1997). A study by Ebener and Irby looked at supportive parenting behaviors of academically successful children from low-income families from the parents', teachers', and children's perspectives. They found three main factors related to success in school.

First, the parents tended to instill the importance of education in their children and how it related to success later in life. They set high expectations for school, saved money for the children's education, and acquired education themselves so as to serve as role models for the children.

Second, the parents created a home environment that was similar to the characteristics, patterns, and behaviors of a school. The parents often read to their children, engaged in problem-solving behaviors, monitored television, and exposed the children to different learning experiences.

Last, the parents ensured the exchange of information between school and home by being actively involved in school programs, volunteering in the classroom, and regularly meeting with teachers.

While these behaviors sound good, they may not be very realistic for some Latino parents. As was discussed earlier, language barriers may inhibit Latino parents' involvement with school activities and teachers. Also, some Latinos with traditional cultural values may not deem it their place to involve themselves in the classroom. Of course, poverty may inhibit the Latino parent from acquiring his or her own education and from saving for a child's college education. And, as was discussed, there may not be enough time to read and spend time with each child due to work hours and large families.

However, the human service worker, whether a teacher, counselor, or social worker, should not give up on this population. There is no doubt that education is paramount to getting out of poverty and increasing one's standard of living. Education also reduces the incidence of other problems, such as domestic violence, child abuse, drug abuse, and crime. All of those who engage with low-income Spanish-speaking clients must share the results of research and educate parents about the value of education in an effort to encourage more parental involvement. Of course, there will be resistance to change, but it will benefit the children. We need to remind the parents that the reason they live in this country is to create a better life for their family and that education is the key to this goal. Explain that in the U.S. there is a history of immigrants who worked hard so their children could attend college and improve their standard of living. During the first big migration in the early 1900s, many Europeans who couldn't speak English came to the U.S. without any education and held low-paying manual jobs. Many children of these immigrants went on to be college educated and hold professional positions. This pattern is possible for the Latino immigrant, as well. Knowing this history might instill hope in the parents for their own children.

HIGH SCHOOL DROPOUTS

If the Latino population does not receive some form of support and encouragement from teachers and other human service workers, they run the risk of becoming high school dropouts. Unfortunately, as a group, Hispanics lag behind the rest of the country in educational attainment. In 1997, 87% of all young adults (ages 25-29) had completed high school. Only 62% of young Hispanic adults had completed high school. Of those 62% who graduated from high school, only 11% graduated from college, compared to 28% of the general population. More disturbing, in 1996, about 30% of Hispanics had not completed high school (National Center for Education Statistics, 1998).

Research determined that there was a difference in dropout rates between first-, second-, and third-generation Latinos. Second-generation students had lower odds of overall dropout, while first- and second-generation students who made it through the first two years of high school were less likely to drop out than were third-generation students. Family income and past academic performance were also associated with the risk of dropping out of high school.

This sad reality of high drop out rates must encourage human service workers to focus on prevention. Without even a high school education, poverty among this population will continue. And along with poverty comes a variety of other problems, as has been shown.

COLLEGE EDUCATION AND LATINOS

Human service workers must also deal with keeping Latinos in college. Many special programs have been created to assist students who may at risk for college dropout. Human service workers can assist these students by counseling them and encouraging them to persist in their college studies.

In a study of Latino students at a local city college (Creason, 1994), the subjects of a survey revealed several factors that they perceived to lead to either academic success or failure. Two of the most important factors have been presented prior: support from the family and an understanding of the long-term satisfaction and career opportunities that a college education can provide. Also, students who declare a major are more likely to graduate than those who do not. Not surprisingly, language acquisition also plays a significant role in educational success. When students are taught in a language other than the one they speak at home, they have more difficulty in school. This fact explains why immigrants and first-generation students demonstrate less academic success than second- and third-generation Latinos.

Other factors reported to be significant to Latinos' college success included financial support, student involvement in extracurricular college activities, and interactions with faculty outside of class. Perhaps the latter two factors can be explained by the Latino need for personalismo. Faculty mentoring may be especially important for the Latino college student, so advisors and counselors should keep this in mind.

Brower, (1992), also encourages college students to get involved in the college environment to prevent dropout. **Social integration** is key to a student perceiving him- or herself as part of the college community, and students who feel socially integrated are more likely to meet the high demands required of college students. This theory about college persistence as related to student integration was tested by Cabrera, Nora, & Castaneda (1993). They wished to explore the idea that **student retention** was based on student commitment to an educational goal and commitment to remain with the institution. This commitment was theorized to be due to a match between the student's motivation and academic ability and the institution's academic and social characteristics. The results of their study indicate that the primary factor leading to college persistence was student intent to persist. Other significant factors included student grade point average, institutional commitment, encouragement, and goal commitment. Advisors and other counselors may use this knowledge when counseling Latino college students and setting up plans to help students remain in college.

ACCOMMODATING ESL STUDENTS IN THE UNIVERSITY

(This section is a partial reprint of Kanel's 2004 article of the same name published in the NEA Higher Education Journal, volume XIX, Number 2, pages 61-68.)

"A recent study shows that one of every three students in school is of a racial or ethnic minority, and that one in seven students between the ages of 5 and seventeen speak a language other than English at home, and more than one third are limited English proficiency. In this section, the term ESL (English as Second Language) is used rather than limited English proficiency to refer to those individuals whose ability to speak English is limited or poor. In some areas, the amount of Hispanic children (many who are ESL students) entering schools outnumbers the number of Whites. Hopefully, some of these students will some day enroll in colleges and universities. However, many will not become proficient in English even by the time they reach college. Other Latino college students enter

American universities without having gone through the American K-12 schools and have very limited English skills. This puts them at a definite disadvantage in a university setting.

University culture often inhibits these students from completing their degrees, thereby reducing the number of ESL students entering professions in which they are needed. Professions such as counseling, social work and teaching are in dire need of college graduates that can speak Spanish and other foreign languages to serve the growing multicultural population in the U.S. as was previously shown in chapters 1 and 3. These American residing Latinos as well as other ethnic minorities such as Vietnamese and middle Easterners need services provided by professionals trained at university settings. Common sense tells us that Latinos that speak Spanish and understand the culture (or Asians that speak Vietnamese, etc.) could provide the types of services needed by this group more effectively than those not familiar with the culture and language. Unfortunately, many of these "would be" professionals do not succeed in university settings because of university academic standards and other organizational cultural characteristics that hamper the academic success of ESL students, despite the fact that they possess the skills necessary for successful employment performance in these service professions.

It may be time to modify standards, particularly in fields in which service to ethnic minorities is the focus. Usually, workers of similar ethnic background provide these services most effectively. Unfortunately, despite Affirmative Action efforts, minorities at universities often do not perform well under traditional academic standards, and are subsequently denied entrance into graduate programs where they are greatly needed. It is at the graduate level that workers in the helping professions have decision-making responsibilities and privileges that allow them to create and implement social programs that would benefit ethnic minorities.

Because the university programs that focus on helping professions are more service-learning oriented than traditional academic programs, standards must be created that assess for successful employment performance rather than assessing for American culturally biased skills such as critical thinking, grammar, and articulation.

Rethinking academic standards will be a challenge for university cultures as academic standards have long been considered a cornerstone in a strong educational system. After all, they were set up in order to provide accountability and ensure educational equity for all learners. They also help guide students and teachers toward learning goals. It is not a novel concept to have both content and performance standards. However, typical performance standards require students to write out their knowledge rather than perform their knowledge. I am suggesting that performance standards should be modified to assess the students' ability to perform an action or service required by a particular position found at helping agencies. For example, I teach a course in which students learn how to conduct crisis intervention interviews. Students are graded on an actual interview that they conduct with another student role-playing a client. The criteria used for evaluation have been developed by researching what counselors in the community do when conducting crisis intervention sessions. I believe that if a student can demonstrate the skills utilized successfully by those employed in the field, then the student deserves to receive an A in this course, even if their English skills as demonstrated on written exams are not good. Even the EEOC (Equal Employment Opportunity Commission) suggests that applicants for jobs or for promotion be rated on criterion shown to be related to successful job performance. Why then, can't we university professors evaluate our students on their ability to demonstrate skills that are necessary for successful job performance rather than skills necessary to pass the GRE or write a journal article?

Most educational cultures and teachers do not reject accommodations for learning-disabled students and may not openly reject accommodations for ESL students. However, many teachers often have very little understanding of language development and may not be equipped to work with students whose language skill levels and intellectual potential are vastly disparate. Developing effective accommodations for such a large number of students would need funding that may not be easily forthcoming. The reality is that these students at some point in their lives will be in the job market, and educators must find ways to ensure they receive the education that meets their unique learning styles. Don't all people in our society deserve to fulfill their full potential? Without accommodations, many students will not have the chance to do this. This was the reason behind accommodating disabled people in the first place. What is wrong with accommodating other types of students who learn differently? We've accepted that a blind student should be allowed to have his text read aloud to him or translated into Braille. Why can't a Latino ESL student have his or her text translated into Spanish or read aloud? Don't we educators really just want our students to learn, grow, and develop skills for a successful and rewarding career?

Accommodating students is not without its debates. Very little research is available that clearly specifies exactly how to accommodate without affecting the skills being assessed. Optimally, an accommodation should only remove construct-irrelevant variance for students with disabilities and have no effect for students without disabilities. There is certainly a need for research that answers questions about the validity of test results for students with a variety of disabilities using a variety of accommodations.[7] This type of research should include accommodations for ESL students as well. As long as non-disabled and non-ESL students aren't unfairly disadvantaged by accommodations, why should anyone care if ESL students are assisted to complete their academic program? There is certainly a need for ESL community workers who are college educated. Often, agencies depend on bilingual, paraprofessionals with no college preparation, and the populations being served at these agencies do not receive effective services because there is no one available who both speaks their language and who has the knowledge base required to provide appropriate services.

Researching these proposed accommodations requires cooperation from schools, however. Although schools purport to offer unlimited possibilities for social advancement, they simultaneously maintain structures that severely limit the probability of advancement for those at the bottom of the social scale[8] often ESL students. As much as we would like to think of schools as being impartial settings, it is probable that built into the fabric of school culture are curricular, pedagogical and evaluative practices that privilege the affluent, white and male segments of society. Hogan-Garcia (1999) refers to theses biases as organizational culture and proposes that it reflects the national culture, which is often incongruent with the cultural backgrounds of many ESL students. The challenge for university systems is to expand the notion of what a 'proper' college education is and rethink old standards that emphasize critical thinking in English, writing formal essays in English, and articulating in a standardized manner in English. These traditional standards may not be relevant for those entering the helping professions where developing human relationships and emotional connection are the essential skills for students to learn.

In addition to the effects of organizational culture on ESL students, they also must contend with the stress of having to speak and listen to a foreign language in front of others. This causes anxiety, which can hinder learning and self-esteem. The student may have the capacity to understand the material and even perform skills necessary for a counseling job, but would be discouraged because of emotional stress. This is similar to the type of anxieties experienced by students suffering from ADD (Attention Deficit Disorder), Dyslexia, or other recognized learning disorders. These students receive special accommodations such as having longer periods to take exams, having someone take notes for them, having interpreters, having texts read to them, and the use of dictionaries during exams. Why can't these same accommodations be available to ESL students?

Other solutions in helping ESL students succeed academically have been offered, but they rely on instructors being willing to put forth effort. College professors must think out of the traditional "box" and move into the needs of the 21st century. After all, we adapted when it came time to accept distance learning, Internet usage, and accommodating the needs of the disabled. Realizing that there is a significant need for ESL college graduates to meet the needs of a multicultural society is the motivating incentive for socially conscious professors.

Villegas & Lucas (2002) have developed a model in preparing culturally responsive instructors. University professors can incorporate these ideas as a way of assisting ESL college students. First, teachers must systematically infuse multicultural issues throughout the curriculum, including the cultural issues facing the students in the class. Often, multicultural issues are discussed as related to consumers of health care and human services. It wouldn't be a large leap for the professor to engage in open dialogue with ESL students about their cultural needs as a student in the course. This material would only help the other students truly understand cultural issues.

They further propose that truly culturally responsive teachers are socioculturally conscious, recognizing that there are multiple ways of perceiving reality, and that these ways are influenced by one's location in the social order. This is not enough, however. The instructor must have an affirming view of students from diverse backgrounds and see these differences as resources for learning rather than a problem to overcome. Teachers must also see themselves as responsible for and capable of bringing about change to make schools more equitable and responsive to all students. It would also help if professors knew about the lives of their students and designed instruction to build on what their students already know while stretching them beyond the familiar. Acknowledging that ESL students already know a great deal and have had experiences and concepts that can help fellow classmates expand their learning is a big part in accommodating these students. Other accommodations include using pertinent examples and analogies from the ESL students' lives to introduce and clarify new concepts. Professors should also take some extra time with these students and guide them into using strategies they can use to monitor their own learning, and help them set high performance expectations that are realistic. Lastly, ESL student anxiety can be reduced by making them aware that fluency in a foreign language takes several years and that practice and study helps considerably in this regard. If professors are willing to engage in candid discussions about the special issues facing ESL students, it might relieve many of the emotional stresses these student encounter as college students, thereby increasing the likelihood of successful completion of college degrees.

This type of frankness may be a bit risky in this politically correct era, but maybe we need to take this risk in order to ensure that all segments of our society are represented in the helping professions. Some of these ideas may even be relevant to other areas as well. For example, many ESL students have excelled in math and engineering courses because they don't require communication skills. Many brilliant scientists might be discouraged if standards required more verbal and communication skills of those students.

A good example might be policies about make-up exams. Some professors will not bend on this policy. This could hinder many Latino college students who are often responsible for driving family members to Mexico when a relative dies or has fallen ill. Is it fair to ask a student to choose between an exam and his or her family? Would it be fair to ask a hearing impaired student to give an oral speech and them mark him down because his voice was not audible?

For decades universities have accommodated students with disabilities because it is believed that they should contribute to society, and so it is justifiable to accommodate them so they can earn a college degree. One cannot argue against the fact that ESL students are also needed in society. Is it not justifiable then to accommodate them as well? (Kanel, 2004)

These articles were used in the writing of the above article:

Casado, M. A., & Dereshiwsky, M. I. (2001). Foreign language anxiety of university students. *College Student Journal, 35*, 4, 539(13).

Coleman, N. L. (2001). Special Needs. (the Twenty-First Century Classroom). *National Forum, 81*, 4, 50(10).

Giacobbe, A. C., Livers, A. F. Jr., Thayer-Smith, R., & Walther-Thomas. (2001). Raising the Academic Standards Bar. *Journal of Disability Policy Studies, 12*, 1, 10(15).

Gittelsohn, J., & Godines, V. (1999, April 4). Redefining school lines. *Orange County Register.* p. 1, 6-7.

Hogan-Garcia, M. (1999). *The Four Skills of Cultural Diversity Competence.* Pacific Grove, CA: Brooks/Cole.

Johnson, E. S. (2000). The effects of accommodations of performance assessments. *Remedial and Special Education, 21*, 5, 261(15).

Mental Health Association of Los Angeles. (1997). *Human resource needs assessment: Human services industry.* Los Angeles: Author.

U.S. Census Bureau. (2001). *Race, Hispanic or Latino.* Available from **www.census.gov**.

Villegas, A. M., & Lucas, T. (2002). Preparing culturally responsive teachers: rethinking the curriculum. *Journal of Teacher Education, 53*, 1, 20(13).

CONCLUSION

Based on all the theories and research, it seems clear that the role of education in the life of Latinos must be emphasized in ways that it has not been traditionally. If we desire to decrease the poverty levels—hence other social problems—of this group, we must be proactive in encouraging higher educational attainment of Hispanics. Teachers, counselors, and other human service workers have an opportunity to spread information to Latinos that helps them understand how education will increase their standard of living. It must be shown, however, that family obligations and other cultural traditions do not have to be sacrificed completely by doing so. True, there will be some sacrifices, but this type of sacrificing for the betterment of one's children has been a historical fact of all immigrant groups throughout U.S. history. In fact, we can show traditional Latino parents that their children will be better prepared to take care of them by getting a college education. Perhaps, some traditional Latino parents may resist their children attending college for fear of losing control over them and fear of lack of contact with them. Human service workers can help by explaining this doesn't have to be the case. In fact, by holding a motivated child back from college, the parents might be inadvertently creating resentment in their child, so he or she won't want to affiliate with them in the future. Children whose parents support them throughout their young adult life may be more prone to voluntarily affiliate with their parents as they move into adulthood. We must be creative in our communications so that we reduce resistance to new ways of living. Please, keep in mind traditional cultural values as you help Spanish-speaking families adopt new values!

GLOSSARY OF TERMS

Cognitive Competence: the level of intellectual capacity that someone has developed, which includes reading abilities, problem-solving skills, and mathematical skills.

Maternal Responsivity: the way in which a mother listens and communicates with a child, how she meets his or her needs, and how she cares for him or her.

Social Integration: how much a student feels a part of the campus and social environment of a school.

Socioeconomic Status: the level of income that someone earns.

Student retention: whether students complete school or drop out.

REFERENCES

Bradley, R. H., & Caldwell, B. M. (1980). The relation of home environment, cognitive competence, and IQ among males and females. *Child Development, 51,* 1140-1148.

Brower, A. M. (1992). The second half of student integration. *Journal of Higher Education, 63,* 4, 441-460.

Cabrera, A. F., Nora, A., & Castaneda, M. B. (1993). College persistence. *Journal of Higher Education, 64,* 2, 123-137.

California Cities, Towns, and Counties: Basic Data Profiles for all Municipalities and Counties. (1990). Palo Alto, CA: Info. Publications.

Connell, P., Spencer, M. B., & Aber, L. (1994). Educational risk and Resilience in Latin-American Youth: Context, Self, Action, and Outcomes in School. *Child Development, 65,* 493-506.

Creason, P., (1994). *An analysis of success indicators for Latino students at Long Beach City College.* A report published by Long Beach City College, CA.

Ebener, R., Lara-Alecio, R., & Irby, B. J. (1997). *Supportive practices among low-income parents of academically successful elementary students in even start programs.* Report published by the Even Start Program.

Kanel, Kim (2000b). Special challenges Japanese Learners of English Face. *The JASEC Bulletin, 9,* 1, 43.

National Center for Education Statistics. (1998). *The Condition of Education.* Washington, D.C.: U.S. Department of Education.

QUESTIONAIRE: PERCEIVED MENTAL HEALTH NEEDS OF LATINOS IN ORANGE COUNTY

Por favor de poner circulo alrededor de la respuesta mas correcta.

1. Mi primera idioma es:
   a. espanol   b. ingles   c. otra _____

2. En su casa, cual idioma se habla mas?
   a. espanol   b. ingles c. los dos igualmente
   d. otra_____

3. Naci en:
   a. Mexico   b. USA   c. otra_____

4. Cuantos anos tiene Ud.?
   a. 18-25   b. 26-35   c. 36-45   d. 46-55   e. 56-65

5. Soy:
   a. casado(a)   b. soltero(a)   c. divorciado(a)
   d. vivo con novio sin casarme

6. Cuantos hijos tiene Ud.?
   a. 1   b. 2   c. 3   d. 4   e. 5
   f. 6   g. Mas que 6   h. Ningunos

7. Por cuantos anos ha vivido en el USA?
   a. 1-3   b. 4-7   c. 8-10   d. 10-15
   e. mas que 15 anos

8. Describe su nivel de hablar el ingles.
   a. bien   b. asi, asi   c. mal

9. Haria Ud. una cita con un terapista familiar si tendria unos problemas de la familia?
   a. si   b. no

10. Si la respuesta fue si, que tipo de problemas son los mas tipico en su familia?(Por favor de poner circulo alrededor de todos que aplican a su familia)
    a. problemas con hijos en escuela
    b. problemas con hijos en bandas
    c. problemas con hijos que no obedecen a los padres
    d. problemas del matrimonio
    e. problemas de drogas o alcohol.

11. Si la respuesta fue no, porque no? (Ponga circulo alrededor de todos que aplican)
    a. tengo miedo de ver una terapista
    b. no se como usar servicios de salud mental
    c. no puedo costar los servicios de terapista
    d. mi seguranza no cubre servicios para salud mental
    e. preferia hablar con familia, amigos o pastor o padre de mis problemas
    f. preferia irme a una botanica y usar medicina
    g. tengo verguenza de ver una terapista

12. Haria Ud. una cita con un psicologo(a) por problemas emocionales los cuales Ud. solamente sufren?
    a. si   b. no

13. Si la respuesta fue si, que tipo de problemas son tipicos para Ud.? (Ponga circulo alrededor de todos que aplican)
    a. depresion   b. los nervios   c. corraje no bajo su control
    d. anciedad   e. problemas con drogas o alcohol

14. Si la respuesta fue no, porque no?(Ponga circulo alrededor de todos que apli-
    can)
    a. tengo miedo de ver psicologo
    b. no se como usar servicios de salud mental
    c. no tengo seguranza que cubre servicios de salud mental
    d. no tengo tiempo para irme
    e. tengo verguenza en irme
    f. solo los locos van a psicologos
    g. preferia irme a mi doctor por medicina
    h. preferia irme a una botanica
    i. Preferia hablar con amigos o familia

15. Para sentirse Ud. los mas comodo, como debe ser un consejero or psicologo?
    (Ponga circulo alrededor de todos que aplican)
    a. muy callado
    b. muy hablado
    c. que da muchos consejos
    d. que pregunta mucha
    e. muy personal
    f. muy profesional

16. Ud. cree que en hablar de su ninez le ayudara en resolver sus problemas de
    hoy dias?
    a. si   b. no

17. En una visita con un consejero, yo preferia hablar de:
    a. sus problemas de hoy dias   b. dificultades de mi ninez

18. Ud. cree que una medicina puede ayudar con problemas de la salud mental?
    a. Si   b. no

19. Para resolver mis problemas emocionales, yo preferia:
    a. tomar medicina   b. hablar con terapista

20. Ud. cree que hay bastante terapistas quienes hablan Espanol?
    a. si   b. no

ENGLISH TRANSLATION OF SURVEY

Please circle the most correct response:

1. My primary language is:
   a. Spanish   b. English   c. other_____

2. In your home, which language is spoken the most?
   a. Spanish   b. English   c. both equally
   d. other_____

3. I was born in:
   a. Mexico   b. USA   c. Other_____

4. How old are you?
   a. 18-25   b. 26-35   c. 36-45   d. 46-55   e. 56-65

5. I am:
   a. married   b. single   c. divorced
   d. living with a significant other

6. How many children do you have?
   a. 1   b. 2   c. 3   d. 4   e. 5
   f. 6   g. more than 6   h. none

7. How many years have you lived in the USA?
   a. 1-3   b. 4-7   c. 8-10   d. 11-15
   e. more than 15

8. Describe your level of speaking English.
   a. good   b. so, so c. bad

9. Would you make an appointment with a family therapist if you had family problems?
   a. yes   b. no

10. If your response was yes, what type of problems are typical in your family? (Please circle all that apply)
    a. problems with your children at school
    b. problems with your children in gangs
    c. problems with your children not obeying their parents
    d. problems in your marriage
    e. problems with drugs or alcohol

11. If your response was no, why not? (Please circle all that apply)
    a. I am afraid to see a therapist
    b. I don't know how to utilize mental health services
    c. I can't afford to see a therapist
    d. My insurance doesn't cover mental health services
    e. I prefer to talk to family, friends, a pastor or clergy about my problems
    f. I prefer to go to a botanical shop and use medicine
    g. I am ashamed to see a therapist

12. Would you make an appointment with a psychologist for emotional problems that you individually suffer from?
    a. yes   b. no

13. If your answer was yes, what type of problems would be typical for you? (Please circle all that apply)
    a. depression   b. general nervousness   c. out of control anger
    d. anxiety   e. drug or alcohol problems

14. If your response was no, why not? (Please circle all that apply)
    a. I am afraid to see a psychologist
    b. I don't know how to use mental health services
    c. I don't have insurance that covers mental health services
    d. I don't have time to go
    e. I am ashamed to go
    f. Only crazy people see psychologists
    g. I prefer to go to my doctor for medicine
    h. I prefer to go to a botanical shop
    i. I prefer to talk with friends or family

15. In order to feel the most comfortable, how would you like a counselor or psychologist to be with you? (Put a circle around all that apply)
    a. very quiet
    b. very talkative
    c. gives a lot of advice
    d. asks a lot of questions
    e. very personal
    f. very professional

16. Do you believe that talking about your childhood will help you resolve your current problems?
    a. yes   b. no

17. In a counseling session, would you prefer to talk about
    a. your current problems   b. your problems from childhood

18. Do you believe that medicine can help you with your mental health problems?
    a. yes   b. no

19. To resolve my emotional problems, I would prefer
    a. to take medicine   b. speak to a therapist

20. Do you believe there are enough therapists who speak Spanish?
    a. yes   b. no

QUESTIONAIRE OF THERAPISTS WHO WORK WITH SPANISH-SPEAKING FAMILIES IN ORANGE COUNTY

1. What best describes your ethnic background?
   a. Hispanic   b. Caucasian   c. African-American
   d. Asian   e. other

2. What is your highest educational degree?
   a. Ph.D   b. M.S./M.A.   c. B.S./B.A.   d. A.A.
   e. no formal degree

3. What type of license or certificate do you hold?
   a. Psychologist   b. LMFT   c. LCSW   d. Psychiatrist
   e. other_____

4. What best applies to you? (regarding Spanish as the language and culture)
   a. Bilingual/Bicultural   b. Bilingual   c. Bicultural
   d. Neither bilingual or bicultural

5. Where do you see clients? (Circle all that apply)
   a. private practice   b. managed care facility
   c. non-profit agency   d. county mental health or other county facility

6. Approximately how many Spanish-speaking clients do you serve a year?
   a. 0-5   b. 6-10   c. 11-15   d. 16-20   e. 21-25
   f. more than 25

7. What are the issues that your Spanish-speaking clients present at the initial counseling session?

   a._____

   b._____

   c. _____

   d._____

8. What type of interventions do you implement with Spanish-speaking clients?

    a._____

    b._____

    c. _____

    d. _____

9. Did your formal education address these issues and interventions adequately?
    a. yes   b. no

10. How would you describe the type of relationship you develop with your Spanish-speaking clients?
    a. personal
    b. anonymous
    c. highly professional
    d. friendly but objective
    e. strictly doctor-patient

11. How does your work with Spanish-speaking clients differ from your work with English-speaking clients?

    a. _____

    b. _____

12. Do you conduct counseling sessions in Spanish?
    a. yes   b. no

13. Do you believe there are enough Spanish-speaking counselors in Orange County to meet the mental health needs of the Spanish-speaking population?
    a. yes   b. no

APPENDIX B

ATAQUE DE NERVIOS QUESTIONNAIRES

Survey for Latinos

Thank you for your participation in this survey. All responses are confidential. You may skip any item or stop taking this survey at any time.

Please circle the most appropriate response.

1. Age
   a. 18-24
   b. 25-35
   c. 36-50
   d. 51-62

2. Gender (researcher assistant will circle if giving survey orally)
   a. male
   b. female

3. Place of birth
   a. United States
   b. Mexico
   c. Central America
   d. South America
   e. Cuba
   f. Puerto Rico
   g. other

4. Ethnic identification
   a. American
   b. Mexican-American
   c. Latino(a)
   d. Hispanic
   e. Other

5. Education
   a. Less than 8 years
   b. Completed high school
   c. Some high school
   d. College degree
   e. Some college

6. Years living in the United States
   a. 1-5
   b. 6-10
   c. 11-15
   d. 16-20
   e. 21 or more years

7. Marital status
   a. Married
   b. Divorced
   c. Separated
   d. Single

8. Have you or someone you know ever experienced "Ataque De Nervios" or heard of it?
   a. yes
   b. no

9. If no, you may turn in your survey now. Thank you for your time. If yes, please continue if you wish.

10. If yes to 8, please describe "Ataque de Nervios" in your own words.

11. What did you or the person you knew do to overcome this problem?
    (Circle all that apply)
    a. Went to a therapist
    b. Got medication from a medical doctor (Please specify what mediction)
    _____
    c. Got psychiatric medication from a psychiatrist (Please specify what
       medication)_____
    d. Went to a curandero at a botanica (Please specify what treatment)
    _____
    e. Talked to family or friends
    f. It went away by itself (How long did it last?)_____
    g. Other

12. What do you think causes "Ataque De Nervios"? (Circle all that apply)
    a. Family conflict
    b. Work conflict
    c. Poor physical health
    d. Emotional problems
    e. Mental illness
    f. Possession by a demon or the devil
    g. A curse or spell put on you by someone else
    h. Being a bad person
    i. Other (Please specify)
    _____

13. Please circle all the complaints, behaviors, or symptoms that you perceive
    as being part of "Ataque de Nervios."
    a. depressed mood most of the day (e.g., sad, empty, tearful)
    b. diminished interest or pleasure in all or almost all activities most of the
       day, nearly every day
    c. significant weight loss or weight gain
    d. insomnia or oversleeping
    e. severe agitation or very slowed down
    f. fatigue or loss of energy nearly every day
    g. feelings of worthlessness or guilt
    h. diminished ability to think or concentrate, or indecisiveness
    i. recurrent thoughts of death, recurrent suicidal ideation or attempt

14. Please circle all the complaints, behaviors or symptoms that you perceive as being part of "Ataque de Nervios."
    a. palpitations, pounding heart, or accelerated heart rate
    b. sweating
    c. trembling or shaking
    d. sensations of shortness of breath or smothering
    e. feelings of choking
    f. chest pain or discomfort
    g. nausea or abdominal distress
    h. feeling dizzy, unsteady, lightheaded, or faint
    i. feelings of unreality or being detached from oneself
    j. fear of losing control or going crazy
    k. fear of dying
    l. numbness or tingling sensations
    m. chills or hot flushes

15. Please circle all the complaints, behaviors, or symptoms that you perceive as being part of "Ataque de Nervios."
    a. excessive anxiety and worry for more days than not for at least 6 months
    b. difficulty in controlling the worry
    c. restlessness or feeling on edge
    d. being easily fatigued
    e. difficulty concentrating or mind going blank
    f. irritability
    g. muscle tension
    h. sleep disturbance

16. Is there anything else you can say about "Ataque de Nervios"?

    _____

    _____

    _____

ATAQUE DE NERVIOS QUESTIONNAIRES

Survey for Therapists and Psychiatrists

Thank you for taking time to complete this survey. The results may prove to be useful in helping mental health providers and physicians understand and treat "Ataque de Nervios" more effectively. Participants may skip any question, or discontinue if they feel uncomfortable answering the questions.

Please circle the most appropriate response.

1. License type
   a. LMFT
   b. LCSW
   c. Psychologist
   d. Psychiatrist
   e. No license

2. Place where you provide service
   a. County behavioral health
   b. Non-profit agency
   c. Managed care facility
   d. Private practice
   e. Residential facility
   f. Other social welfare or services

3. Are you bilingual in Spanish and English?
   a. yes
   b. no

4. Are you bicultural Latino and American?
   a. yes
   b. no

5. How many Spanish-speaking clients do you see in a year?
   a. 0-5
   b. 6-10
   c. 11-15

d. 16-20
e. 21-25
f. 25+

6. Have you seen clients or spoken with other helping professionals about clients who complain of "Ataque de Nervios"?
    a. yes
    b. no

7. If no, you may turn in your questionnaire now. Thank you for your time.

8. If yes, how many cases of "Ataque de Nervios" have you dealt with?
    a. 0-3
    b. 4-6
    c. 7-9
    d. 10-12
    e. 13+

9. How would you formally label the phenomenon called "Ataque de Nervios"?
    a. Major depressive episode
    b. Generalized anxiety disorder
    c. Panic disorder
    d. Other (Please list)_____

10. What do you believe causes "Ataque de Nervios"? (Circle all that apply)
    a. family conflict
    b. biochemical imbalance
    c. intrapsychic conflicts
    d. childhood abuse
    e. immaturity
    f. drugs and alcohol abuse
    g. other_____

11. What is your treatment approach for "Ataque de Nervios"? (Circle all that apply)
    a. Medication (type)_____
    b. Cognitive therapy

c. Supportive therapy

d. Expressive therapy

e. Psychoanalytic therapy

f. Family therapy

12. Should Ataque de Nervios be listed as a separate diagnosis in the DSM?
    a. yes
    b. no

13. Please circle all the complaints, behaviors, or symptoms that you perceive
    as being part of "Ataque de Nervios."
    a. depressed mood most of the day (e.g., sad, empty, tearful)
    b. diminished interest or pleasure in all or almost all activities most of the
    day, nearly every day
    c. significant weight loss or weight gain
    d. insomnia or oversleeping
    e. severe agitation or very slowed down
    f. fatigue or loss of energy nearly every day
    g. feelings of worthlessness or guilt
    h. diminished ability to think or concentrate, or indecisiveness
    i. recurrent thoughts of death, recurrent suicidal ideation or attempt

14. Please circle all the complaints, behaviors, or symptoms that you perceive
    as being part of "Ataque de Nervios."
    a. palpitations, pounding heart, or accelerated heart rate
    b. sweating
    c. trembling or shaking
    d. sensations of shortness of breath or smothering
    e. feelings of choking
    f. chest pain or discomfort
    g. nausea or abdominal distress
    h. feeling dizzy, unsteady, lightheaded, or faint
    i. feelings of unreality or being detached from oneself
    j. fear of losing control or going crazy
    k. fear of dying
    l. numbness or tingling sensations
    m. chills or hot flushes

15. Please circle all the complaints, behaviors or symptoms that you perceive as being part of "Ataque de Nervios."
    a. excessive anxiety and worry for more days than not for at least 6 months
    b. difficulty in controlling the worry
    c. restlessness or feeling on edge
    d. being easily fatigued
    e. difficulty concentrating or mind going blank
    f. irritability
    g. muscle tension
    h. sleep disturbance

Thank you

APPENDIX C

ENGLISH TO SPANISH DICTIONARY

Numbers
1: uno   2: dos 3: tres 4: cuatro 5: cinco 6: seis 7: siete 8: ocho 9: nueve 10: dies
11:once 12: doce 13: trece 14: catorce 15: quince 16: dies y seis 17: dies y siete
18: dies y ocho 19: dies y nueve 20 : viente 30: treinta 40: cuarenta 50: cincuenta
60: seisenta 70: setenta 80: ochenta 90: noventa 100: cien 1000: mil

Days of the week
Mon: Lunes Tues: Martes Wed: Miercoles Thur: Jueves Fri: viernes
Sat: Sabado Sun: Domingo

Months of the year
Jan: Enero Feb: Febrero Mar: Marzo Apr: Abril May: Mayo June:Junio
July: Julio August: Agosto Sept: Septiembre Oct: Octubre Nov: Noviembre
Dec: Diciembre

Seasons
Winter: Invierno Spring: Primavera Summer: Verano Fall/Autumn: Otono

Holidays
President's Day: Dia de los Presidentes
Easter: Pascua
Fourth of July: Dia de Independencia
Thanksgiving: Dia de Gracia

Christmas: Navidad
New Year: Ano nuevo

TERMS OFTEN USED IN THE SCHOOL SYSTEM

Absent: Ausente
Add(to): Anadir
Amount: Cantidad
Attend(to): Asistir

Bathroom: Bano
Book: Libro
Bring(to): Traer (Bring me the note=Traigame la carta)

Call(to): Llamar (what are you called?=Como se llama?)
Carpet: Alfombra
Class: Clase
Cold/flu: Gripe
Cough: Tos
Cost: Cuesta
Count(to): Contar (Count with me=Cuentan conmigo)

Desk: Escritorio
Draw(to): Dibujar

Eat(to): Comer (breakfast=desayuno, lunch=almuerzo, dinner=comida)

Fail(to): Fallar
Food: Comida

Get(to): Sacar, recibir(to receive)
Give(to): Dar (give it to me=Damelo
Go(to): Irse, (go!=Vayase!)

Help(to): Ayuda
Hit: Pegar
Home: casa or hogar
Homework: tarea

House: casa
Housework: Obra de casa

Know(to) Saber (I know=yo se, I don't know=no se)

Lack(to): Falter
Letters: Letras
Library: Biblioteca
Line: Linea
Listen(to): Escuchar (Listen to me=Escuchanme!)
Look(to): Mirar (Look at me=Miranme)

Name: Nombre (Write your name=Escribe su nombre, what is your name=Como se llama)
Note: Carta
Notice: Noticia
Number: Numero

Page: Pagina
Paint(to): Pintar
Paper: Papel
Pass(to): Pasar
Pen: Pluma
Pencil: Lapiz
Play(to): Jugar
Please: Por Favor
Put(to): Poner (Put it down=Ponlo abajo!)

Quiet(to be): Callarse (Be quiet=Callase!, Not quiet=inquieto)
Queen: Reina

Read(to): Leer(Read page 2=Lee pagina dos)
Ready: Lista (Are you ready?=Estan Listas?)
Repeat(to): Repitir (Repeat after me=Repiten por favor)

School: Escuela
Sit(to): Sentarse (Sit Down=Sientase!)
Students: Estudiantes/Alumnos

Teach(to): Ensenar
Teacher: Maestro/maestra
Tell(to): Decir (Tell me=digame)
Truth: La Verdad
Try(to): Tratar (Try to do it=Trata de hacerlo)

Water: Agua

TERMS OFTEN USED IN MENTAL HEALTH SETTINGS

Accomplish (to): lograr
Accustomed: Acostumbrado
Afraid: Tener Miedo (I'm afraid: Tengo miedo, Are you afraid?: Tiene miedo?)
Alcohol: Alcohol
Alcoholic: Alcoholico
Alcoholism: Alcoholismo
Angry: Enojado
Anger: Coraje
Anxiety: Anciedad, (Los Nervios is more commonly used to describe a state of suffering from anxiety or depression)
Appointment: Una cita

Bad: Mal, feo/fea
Beliefs: Creencias
Building: El edificio

Call(to): Llamar (a call=una llamada)
Can't: No poder, no puedo(I can't)
Client: Cliente
Confidential: Confidencial
Consequences: Consequencias
Control(to): Controlar, (the control=el control)
Cope(to): lidiar (to deal with children), manejar los problems (to deal with problems)
Counselor: Consejera
Crazy: Loco
Cry: Llorar
Culture: La Cultura

Death: La muerte
Depressed: Deprimida
Difficulty: Dificultad , dificil(hard)
Disability: Desabilidad, incapacidad
Disorder: Desorden
Drunk: Borracho/tomado
Drink(to): Tomar

Employee: Empleado
Employee Assistance Program: Programa Para Ayudar Los Empleados
Evaluation: Evaluacion
Expectation: Esperanza (also means hope)

Family: La familia
Fear: Miedo
Feelings: Sentimientos
Feel(to): Sentir

Hard Life: Vida Dura
Have to: Tiene que, Hay que
Help: Ayuda
Help(to): Ayudar
Hit(to): Pegar, golpear
Hope (to): Esperar
Hour: La Hora

Insurance: Aseguranza, seguro

Late: Tarde
Lonely: Sentir Solo
Loss: Perdido (to lose=perdir)

Mean: Antipatico, cruel, malo
Medicine: La Medicina
Mental Health: Salud Mental
Mental Health Services: Los servicios de salud mental

Needs: Necesidades (emotional needs=necesidades emocionales
Nice: Amable, simpatico (easy to get along with)
Nightmares: Pesadillos

Office: La oficina

Pills: Pastillas
Police: La policia
Power: Poder
Prescription: Receta
Privileges: Privilegios
Problems: Problemas
Process: El Proceso
Psychiatrist: Psiquiatra
Psychologist: Psicologo

Sad: Triste
Sadness: Tristeza
Shame: Verguenza
Sick: Enfermo
Sickness: Enfermedad
Sleep problem: Insomnia
Sleep(to): Dormir
Spousal abuse: Maltratado por el esposo
Suffer(to): Sufrir
Suffering: Sufrimiento
Support: Apoyo

Therapy: Terapia
Therapist: Terapista
Thought: Pensamiento, (beliefs=creencias)
Threat: Amenaza
Threaten(to): Amenazar
Treatment: Tratamiento psiquiatra, Trato
Trust: Confianza
Trust(to): Confiar

TERMS OFTEN USED IN THE SOCIAL WELFARE SYSTEM

Abuse(to): Abusar, (noun= Abuso)
Affection: Carino
Anger: Coraje
Anger: corajudo
Attorney: Abogado
Aunt: Tia
Birthdate: Fecha de Nacimiento
Boyfriend: Novio
Brother: Hermano
Bus: Autobus

Care (to care for): Cuidado, Cuidar, Yo cuido, Ud. cuida, ellos cuidan, nosotros cuidamos
Catholic: Catolico
Change: Cambio(money) Cambiar (to change)
Child abuse: Abuso del nino
Church: Iglesia
Court: Corte
Cousin: Primo(boy) Prima(girl)

Daughter: Hija (often said Mija)
Dead: muerta
Death: Muerte
Discipline: Disciplina

Emotional: Sentimental

Family: Familia
Father: Padre, papa
Father-in-law: Suegro
Fault: Culpa
Force: Fuerza

Girlfriend: Novia
Grandfather: Abuelo
Grandmother: Abuela
Guilty: Culpalble

Homework: Tarea
Housework: Obra de la casa, que hacer
Husband: Esposo, Marido

Law: La Ley
Lawyer: Abogado
Legal: legal
Lover: Amante

Maltreatment: Maltratamiento
Marriage: Matrimonio
Masculine: Machista
Money: Dinero
Mother: Madre, mama
Mother-in-law: Suegra

Neglect(to): Mal criar

Physical: Fisico
Play: Jugar Juego(game)
Poor: Pobre
Poverty: Pobeza
Public: Publico
Punishment: Castigo

Rage: Rabia
Rape(to): Violar (violado)
Relative: Pariente
Rich: Rico

School: La Escuela
Sexual molest: Molestar
Sexual relations: Relaciones
Shame: Verguenza
Social services: Servicio social
Social worker: Trabajador social
Stepmother: Madrasta
Stepfather: Padrasto

Strong: Fuerte

Uncle: Tio

Weak: Debil
Wife: Esposa, Mujer
Work: Trabajo (Trabajar: to work)

INDEX